The Wild Side

STEPHEN R. DATZ

GENERAL TRADE CORPORATION

Copyright © 1990 by Stephen R. Datz

The episodes portrayed in this book are based upon actual incidents. In many cases, characters' names, identities, and other relevant details have been fictionalized to protect individual privacy. Therefore, any resemblance to actual persons, living or dead, locales, or events are purely coincidental.

ISBN: 0-88219-024-5
ISBN-13: 978-0-88219-024-2

Cover design: Mike Jenson
Cover copyright © 1990 Stephen R. Datz
Manufactured in the United States of America

Published by General Trade Corporation
Post Office Box 402
Loveland, Colorado 80539

www.stephenrdatz.com

10 9 8 7 6 5 4 3 2

Philatelic Books by Stephen R. Datz

THE BUYER'S GUIDE

CATALOGUE OF ERRORS ON U.S. STAMPS

THE DATZ PHILATELIC INDEX

ON THE ROAD

STAMP COLLECTING

STAMP COLLECTORS BIBLE

STAMP INVESTING

TOP DOLLAR PAID

THE WILD SIDE

CONTENTS

ACKNOWLEDGMENTS

A great many people assisted in making this book a reality. Special thanks are due John Hotchner, Steven Rod, James Magruder, and Jacques Schiff for taking the time to read preliminary drafts and offer suggestions and criticisms.

Thanks are also due to those kind enough to share their experiences: Chuck Band, Ward Crowley, Max Hickox, Alex Ionnides, Val McDaniel, Joe Neri, Randy Nilson, Jim Peterson, Henry Pobuda, Pat Timm, and Dennis With.

I'm grateful to *The Denver Post* for permission to quote from an article "Pair Held in Baby-Death Probe" that appeared November 12, 1975.

Thanks to Muriel Olson for proofreading and able assistance in helping shape the final draft. And, finally, thanks to ever-patient wife Susan for her proofreading and general suggestions.

AUTHOR'S NOTE

This book is about stamp dealing, or more precisely, the wild side of stamp dealing. The episodes are drawn from my own personal experience and experiences of friends and acquaintances in the stamp trade. The cast includes a host of characters engaged in all manner of mischief: con games, robbery, scams, frauds, even murder. I've also included a section featuring some of the more memorable characters and eccentrics I've run across, even though they're not involved in criminal activity.

Also included are a couple of stories that revolve around coins and coin dealers. In the case of "More Flim-Flam," I found the fraud so outrageous, so perfectly planned and executed, that I thought you'd enjoy it.

My experiences are by no means unique. I'm sure if you take your favorite stamp dealer out to dinner, he'll be more than happy to entertain you well into the night with fascinating anecdotes about the stamp business.

Don't misunderstand, the stamp business is not an endless procession of exciting deals. Mostly it's just routine. The kinds of characters and episodes in this book occur just often enough to keep things fresh and interesting.

Having said that, welcome to *The Wild Side*.

PART ONE

MURDER & MAJOR CRIME

MURDER MOST FOUL

"He was murdered," Brad Rawlins said, his tone matter of fact, his words ice water in the face.

"Murdered?" I repeated, not because I had misunderstood, but because I found it difficult to grasp the stark reality of Brad's words. I have appraised innumerable estates, but the decedents typically had died of old age, not murder.

"Tortured, then murdered," Brad nodded. "They were after his stamps and coins."

"Murdered for these?" The meager group of covers on my desk hardly justified a simple theft, let alone murder. "Surely there must have been better items that were not recovered."

"No, not really. I'm afraid Charlie had a habit of exaggerating . . . and he talked too much."

It was a bright, warm September morning. Sunshine streamed through the south-facing window of my office. A beautiful day, except for the matter of murder. Brad, a customer and old friend, had phoned the day before to set up an appointment for me to view a collection he'd been entrusted to dispose of by the executor of a friend's estate. The deceased friend's name had been Charlie.

The collection filled a cardboard carton. Brad had parked it beside my desk. Charlie had been fascinated by the Space Shuttle Challenger disaster. He had accumulated a variety of covers and memorabilia, much of it heavily duplicated. I pulled out a fat bundle of 100-200 covers, all postmarked January 28, 1986, the day Challenger had exploded on takeoff.

"He thought the covers would be a good investment," Brad said.

"Apparently so," I replied, "judging by the quantity he bought. Unfortunately, just because they're postmarked Cape Canaveral on the day of the tragedy doesn't make them particularly valuable."

"He liked to send them out for autographs," Brad said. "Got signatures from anyone even remotely connected with the Challenger disaster. Look, there's a whole album full."

The autograph album turned out to be the best item in the collection. It contained dozens of autographed covers, all on envelopes identical to those in the bundle, and each bearing the signature of an important personality related to the space program or the official disaster inquiry.

Another bundle contained 200 first day covers for the 1962 Project Mercury stamp.

I spent a few minutes looking the collection over, then said, "I'm afraid the collection isn't worth much. Lots of heavily duplicated items, autographed to be sure, but not by well-known individuals."

"Well, Charlie wasn't too sophisticated," Brad said. "He just loved to collect things—all sorts of things—and there was no rhyme or reason to what he collected. His house was full of stuff— matchbooks, marbles, beer cans, slot machines, you name it."

"How did it happen?" I asked, my thoughts turning from the covers to the crime. The words *tortured* and *murdered* sounded so unreal.

"Charlie was a young fellow, in his thirties. He lived in a fabulous house on East Sixth Avenue Parkway."

East Sixth Avenue Parkway is an exclusive Denver neighborhood of expensive, stately homes.

"He'd come into some money—quite a lot, actually—which he spent rather freely on his multitude of hobbies. He was a helluva guy, but not particularly knowledgeable. And totally bargain oriented. He'd buy just about anything if the price was right. Unfortunately, all too often his bargains turned out to be sow's ears rather than silk purses.

"He was single and affable. He loved to bar hop, make new friends, and talk about his treasures. He could go on for hours about his shrewd acquisitions, about their rarity and value. I don't think it ever occurred to him that he was boasting.

"The funny thing is, explaining it now makes Charlie sound like a braggart, and maybe he was, but when he was right there in front of you spinning a tale, it came across more as entertainment than boasting. He was that personable, that genuinely fun to listen to."

Brad paused and smiled.

"His adventures were peopled with charmingly eccentric characters in unusual circumstances. They made good listening, and he never ran out of them.

"Stories effervesced from him. He'd get so excited, he'd jump right out of his seat and energetically gesture to emphasize a point. I often thought he should have been on stage.

"He once told me how he outsmarted a museum curator who was bent on acquiring a mineral collection from an estate, a collection they both wanted badly. Charlie described the curator as a squint-eyed, punctilious little parasite possessing a vinegar-and-ice personality, a man who smiled only when it served his purpose. Charlie called him Doctor No. I'm not sure whether Charlie thought it more important to get the collection or to keep Doctor No from getting it.

" 'I saved the collection from that squirrelly little dung-beetle and his black-hole-museum,' Charlie told me later. Those were his exact words. Doctor No had incurred Charlie's ire by referring to him as a cultural buccaneer. The museum lobbied the heirs to donate the collection and take a tax deduction. They further argued that the collection, which had been the father's lifetime work, would be kept intact rather than broken up. As part of the sales pitch, Doctor No painted Charlie as a cultural buccaneer who would break up the collection and profit enormously, even obscenely, in the process.

"I doubt that Charlie would have broken it up. Profit was not his motive. He perceived himself as a gentleman collector in the mold of the grand gentlemen collectors of yesteryear, the men who acquired dinosaur eggs from the Gobi, antiquities from desert tombs south of Cairo, Etruscan frescoes, and the like. He even entertained the grandiose notion that someday he would build a museum to house his collection.

"In any case, the rivalry over the collection created a venomous enmity between Charlie and Doctor No. 'A terrible fate awaited those marvelous specimens, had they fallen into the hands of Doctor No,' he told me. 'They would have wound up in cardboard boxes gathering dust on a storeroom shelf along with all the other stuff he'd conned people out of over the years with his phony, holier-than-thou, in-the-public-interest sales pitch. I've seen the back room of his museum. It's a world-class exhibit of brown cardboard boxes ever so neatly catalogued and numbered. That's great, if you're in the business of exhibiting boxes. I'm not.' "

"Did he get the collection?" I asked.

"Oh, yes, but it was a battle. 'But I beat him at his own game,' Charlie boasted. 'I invited the family over to my home. I showed them my collections. I assured them that their collection would remain intact, that resale for profit was not my motive. Then, I made a cash offer, put the money on the table. They must have liked what they saw and what I said, because we did business.'

"Vinegar and honey," Brad said, wrapping up the tale. "It was a battle between vinegar and honey. And honey won. Charlie could charm the quills off a porcupine—and the cold, hard cash didn't hurt, either. He was thrilled. In his mind, he had performed a great public service. 'The public would have been deprived of seeing those wonderful little gems,' he told me, proud that he'd rescued the collection from the clutches of the rapscallion Doctor No. Yet it's beyond me how his owning the collection benefited the public more than the museum's owning it. However, Charlie never gave a moment's thought to such incongruities. He was supremely self-confident, unselfconsciously egocentric. He marched to the beat of his own drummer—unhesitatingly. That's just the way he was."

Again, Brad paused and smiled.

"Then there's the story of the Black Widow" he continued. 'She reminded me of a black widow,' Charlie told me. 'She was big, plump, and always dressed in black. Her house was infested with cobwebs. Her husband's name had been Johnnie Black. She was the Widow Black,' Charlie laughed, amused by the fact that *widow* could be used either before or after the surname Black.

"She lived alone in a big, old house," Brad said. "The kind they used to build on quarter-block lots around the turn of the century. It sat on a hill in north Denver, surrounded by an antique cast-iron fence overgrown by shrubbery so dense you couldn't see through it. Sitting high on up that hill, the house looked for all the world like the Bates home in the movie *Psycho*.

"Her husband, Johnnie Black, had died years before. Rumor had it that he'd been a prohibition-era bootlegger and that she had a bunch of old slot machines stashed in her basement."

" 'I first learned about her,' Charlie told me, 'from an old-timer spinning tales about the good old days during prohibition. To hear him tell it, the hottest spot in town was Johnnie Black's place: hundred-proof bathtub gin; jazz, by turns as lively as Tabasco jambalaya or as mellow as a Louisiana sunset; gambling, mostly craps and slots; and slender, silky women decked out in elegant evening wear, their diamonds and pearls sparkling in the bluish haze of cigarette smoke, their laughter as rich and smooth as twelve-year-old Scotch.

" 'I thought it was a rumor, barroom folklore,' Charlie told me. 'After all, what would Johnnie Black's widow be doing with all those slots? Naturally, I had to go over and see her. It took several visits to make any headway. At first, she didn't want to talk to me. But I persisted. After several visits the ice began to melt. Even then, she wouldn't talk about Johnnie's business and only referred to the old days in general terms. She wouldn't admit to having any slots. She was scared to death that slot machines were illegal to own, that she'd be in big trouble if anyone found out.'

" 'Eventually,' Charlie said, 'I convinced her that slot machines are legal to own as collector's items. I assured her that if she sold them to me, no one would ever know where they came from. And if that weren't enough, I laid five thousand bucks in cash on her parlor table. Fanned those C-notes out like a deck of cards—my aces in the hole. She looked at the money for quite a while, then asked if I'd like to see the machines before paying for them. Bingo! I knew I had a deal!'

" 'Down the basement we went. God, it was spooky—spider webs covered everything. They got in my hair, stuck to my hands and clothes. I was sure they were black widow webs. I was equally sure one of those fat little spiders would pounce on me or drop down the back of my neck, but none did. The basement looked like the Black Hole of Calcutta. It hadn't been cleaned in years. The only light came from a single, low-watt bulb operated by a pull string. The slots, covered with decades of grime, were piled in a dark, dingy corner, which had once been the coal room. Do you know how many slots I found?' Charlie asked.

"I shrugged," Brad said. "I had no idea.

" 'Thirteen! Can you believe it? Thirteen antique, roaring-twenties, speakeasy slot machines. My eyes bugged right out of my head. I pawed through the pile. They were cruddy but intact, certainly restorable. I was thrilled. "You've got yourself a deal," I told the Widow Black. But before she'd let me take them, she insisted I cover each one in a plastic trash bag so that no one could see what I was hauling off.'

"He had the machines restored," Brad continued, "And on one of them he had black widows painted in place of the lemons. 'I love the look on a person's face when those three little spiders come up on a jackpot,' Charlie delighted in saying, his eyes full of glee.

"Were Charlie's stories true?" Brad asked glancing at me. "Who knows? It really doesn't matter. He made lots of friends in bars around town. Some of them were kind of strange, but that didn't seem to bother him. He was drawn to offbeat people and unusual situations. Unfortunately, he wasn't terribly selective about who he boasted to. One night, the wrong guys were listening. They took his exaggerations at face value.

"They followed him home, bound and gagged him, then demanded his rare coins and stamps. Of course, he couldn't produce anything significant, just the stamps and covers on the desk in front of you. And the coins weren't much better. The other stuff—the matchbooks, marbles, arrowheads—either didn't interest them or, like the slot machines, were too bulky or too heavy to carry off.

"They thought Charlie was holding out on them, that the good stuff was hidden somewhere in his house. So they burned him with cigarettes, cut him with knives or razors, and God knows what else, trying to force him to reveal where the loot was hidden. But there was nothing to reveal. The torture went on all night."

I swallowed hard.

I hefted the bundle of Project Mercury covers, chilled by the icy knowledge that someone had died a slow and terrible death over them.

"Sometime in the early morning hours," Brad continued, "when it became apparent that Charlie had no valuable coins and stamps, the killers forced him to write checks to them, each for several thousand dollars. When he finished, they stabbed him in the back and chest, slit his throat, then took him out and dumped him in a field. A farmer found his body three or four days later.

"And here's the truly odd thing. They used their real names on the checks. Hard to imagine, isn't it?"

"Yes," I replied, struggling with the bizarreness of it. If I were going to murder someone, the last thing I'd do is use my own name on checks I'd forced the victim to write. It was the most inept thing I could imagine. "Didn't they stop to think that the checks, each for several thousand dollars—the last checks written by the victim, dated the day of his death, made out to strangers—was bound to stick out like a sore thumb?"

"They did stick out like a sore thumb," Brad said. "Once investigators became aware of them, they zeroed in on the suspects right away. They staked out their house and arrested them. No muss, no fuss."

"Unbelievable!" I said.

"It's lucky they weren't too bright," Brad said. "Anyway, they were tried and convicted. They're on death row."

Charlie's collection, arrayed before me on my desk, brought home the alarming reality of his murder. I thought about the times I might have spoken with a little too much pride about special stamps I owned. The notion that I had just survived a near miss rushed past like a speeding truck. Suddenly, it seemed an imperatively good idea to keep quiet about my prized possessions. Silence, I reflected, is, indeed, golden.

The sunny, lighthearted mood we had enjoyed during Brad's narration of Charlie's earlier exploits had dissolved. The brutality of his untimely end lingered. Brad had come for an appraisal, and even though we had enjoyed the distraction of Charlie's exploits, the covers on my desk reminded me of the business at hand. I quickly reviewed them again.

"The autographs are the best part of the collection," I said. "I'm sorry to be the bearer of bad news, but whole deal is worth only a few hundred dollars at most. Certainly not worth killing someone for."

"Oh, I don't think Charlie was killed for the covers," Brad said matter-of-factly. "His big mouth killed him."

THE FLIM-FLAM MAN

Although the name J.J. Treadwell didn't immediately ring a bell, Pat Timm was pleased by his phone call.

"We met at APEX a couple of weeks ago," Treadwell said. Pat couldn't place the name or recall a face to go with it. APEX had been busy. She'd met dozens of new people, most of whom she'd quickly forgotten. So she didn't think it unusual that J.J. Treadwell's name didn't come right to mind.

"I'm an attorney down here in Colorado Springs," he explained. "I'm from California but living here temporarily while working on some Defense Department litigation. It seems to drag on and on . . . you know how the government works."

Pat still couldn't recall the name or the man, but she listened anyway. He continued, "I was impressed by you and what others have to say about you. You've a lot of friends who speak very highly of you. I consider myself a good judge of character. I have to be in my line of work, and I can tell that you've got good, old-fashioned integrity."

Pat was flattered. The fact that she couldn't recall Treadwell's name or face grew less important as the conversation progressed.

"I really enjoy stamps, but I'm a very busy man. I just don't have the time to devote to them that I'd like to. I also think stamps happen to be a good investment, and I'd like to begin accumulating some of the better issues."

Treadwell spoke rapidly, succinctly. Pat listened intently. The smooth current of conversation, like that of a shining, swollen mountain stream, began to carry her ever more swiftly downstream.

"That's why I'm looking for someone in the stamp business I can trust," Treadwell said. "Someone I can rely on to provide me with high-quality stamps at fair prices. I'm not a stingy person. However, I expect to be treated fairly."

If there was one thing Pat prided herself on, it was her rock-solid sense of fairness.

"I think you're the dealer I've been looking for," Treadwell said. "In fact, I'm sure of it."

Pat was, too.

"I don't want any junk, only top-quality stamps," Treadwell continued. "The kind that will appreciate. Can you help me out?"

"I'm sure I can," Pat replied.

"Good," Treadwell said. "Uh-oh, gotta go. Got an important call coming in on the other line. I'll get back to you." The call was over just as suddenly as it had begun.

Treadwell's call left Pat with a warm, pleasant feeling. She was flattered by his confidence, pleased with the prospect of an affluent new customer.

Treadwell called back the next day. "I've been thinking about stamps, and I just can't wait to get started. Could you put together a thousand dollar package for me?"

"I'd be happy to," Pat replied. "Anything specific?"

"Like I said, better U.S. stamps—mint Columbians, early airmails, that kind of stuff. I'll leave it to you. Just make sure they're high-dollar items. No cheap stuff."

Treadwell was the kind of customer stamp dealers dream of, an undemanding, liberal spender. Pat began to plan the first shipment aloud. "I've got a beautiful White Plains sheet—"

"That'll be fine," Treadwell interrupted. "No need to go over every item. Just give me a good variety. I've got to be in court in just a couple of minutes, so I'll have to make it short. Let me give you my credit card number. Just charge the stamps, and FedEx them to me here in the Springs." He gave her the credit card number and the address of his hotel.

Pat called the credit card clearing number for an authorization number, and the charge was approved. She selected a small group of premium quality items to go along with the White Plains sheet, paying special attention to quality. Then she sent them on their way. Treadwell would have them the next day.

home phone number and suggested that she follow up. A disturbing thought hit her: What if Bridger was right?

She called Bridger for advice. He eagerly volunteered to call the customer at home.

"Mr. Johnson," Bridger said. "I'm calling about the stamps you ordered from Pat Timm."

"Stamps? What stamps? Who did you say?"

"Pat Timm. The thousand dollars' worth of rare stamps you ordered. I'm just calling to confirm your mailing address."

"I didn't order any rare stamps. I don't know any Pat Timm. Say, what's this all about, anyway?"

"Someone using your name and credit card number called Pat Timm—she's a stamp dealer in Denver, Colorado—and ordered a thousand dollars' worth of rare stamps."

"Well, I don't know the first thing about it. I don't collect stamps, and I sure as heck didn't order any over the phone from Denver, Colorado."

It was just as Bridger suspected—a credit card scam. Pat was shaken when she heard the news. Bridger took charge. He alerted the credit card company, then called the FBI. The FBI instructed Pat to ship a dummy parcel. They would arrest whoever showed up to claim it.

It was a clever con. The crooks obtained credit card numbers from an accomplice, who worked at a filling station in California. The victims all had one thing in common, a single all-important criterion: they carried gold cards. The accomplice simply copied the numbers from their charge slips, then passed them on to his buddies, who made the actual calls.

The crooks used the card numbers to make phone orders for a variety of valuable, highly liquid merchandise. They knew the system intimately. They knew that, if they were careful, they could use a card for a week or two before anyone sounded the alarm. They knew that victims remain unaware that their credit cards are being misused until they receive their monthly statements. They knew that high-dollar charges on gold cards attract less attention than similar charges on non-gold cards. They also knew that a series of moderate charges attracts less attention than one large purchase. That's why they only charged $1,000 at a time. They knew that, because the cards had not been reported stolen, credit card companies would authorize charges to merchants who phoned in to verify purchases. It was all very slick.

The con artists handled deliveries with equal ingenuity. They phoned Los Angeles area hotels and made reservations for arrival a day or two later. They said they were expecting important documents to arrive by FedEx and asked hotels to hold them, pending their arrival. The hotels were happy to oblige. The con men then instructed victims to ship parcels to the street addresses of the hotels. Express delivery couriers stopped at the hotels, checked at front desk, learned that parcels were expected by an arriving guest, and left them. All that remained was for one of the crooks to walk up to the front desk, claim the shipment, and walk out without leaving a trace. It was simple and ingenious.

The next time one of the crooks called, Pat, following FBI instructions, prepared and shipped a dummy package via Express Mail. During the next couple of days, the con man called back several times, wondering why the package hadn't arrived. Pat feigned ignorance. "It should have been there by now," she said. "I don't know why it's not, but I'll try to find out." Pat was stalling, again according to FBI instructions. They didn't want the shipment left at a hotel. They felt it would be easier to arrest the man at the post office.

Finally, Pat told the con man that there had been a mix-up. Either she had made an error in the address or the carrier couldn't find the address. She wasn't exactly sure what happened. In any case, he'd have to pick up the package at the post office.

It should have gone smoothly, but it didn't. According to Pat—and she's not sure what the hitch was—there was a lack of cooperation between the FBI and the Postal Service. Perhaps it was a breakdown in communications, perhaps a jurisdictional dispute, or perhaps the issue of capturing the thief became secondary to who would make the arrest. Whatever the reason, the con artist was never apprehended.

After that, the phone orders abruptly stopped. Pat thought it was all over.

Unfortunately, it wasn't. Pat's shock on discovering that her investment customers were crooks was nothing compared to learning that her bank had deducted $14,000 from her account to offset the fraudulent charges. She couldn't understand why she was being stuck with the loss.

"It's not fair," she complained. "I acted in good faith, called for a charge authorization on each sale, as required. And in each case, authorization was given."

But the bank would have none of it. Their position was that an authorization is 100 percent valid only if the customer is personally known to the merchant. Because the con men weren't personally known to her, the bank asserted that she had accepted the risk of taking payment by credit card. Therefore, she was entirely liable for the fraudulent charges. And so, Pat was left holding the proverbial bag, a $14,000 bag.

Pat's was a small dealer. The $14,000 loss was like a knife through the heart. Pat has since closed the store and now restricts herself to doing business with old friends, people she knows and trusts.

By the way, if you're ever in Denver, and you want to do business with Pat, don't bother asking if she accepts credit cards.

MORE FLIM-FLAM

Although it involves coins rather than stamps, I've included this story because of its ingeniousness and dollar magnitude.

One bright morning a few years back, a well-dressed man entered Cherry Creek Coin in Denver. He inquired about investing in gold bullion coins. He said that he'd be closing a real estate deal in Grand Junction, Colorado, in a couple of weeks. He'd have some cash to invest and was considering putting part of it into precious metals. He was polite, articulate, and sincere. He inquired whether Cherry Creek Coin regularly inventoried enough gold bullion coins to fill a $15,000 order on short notice. Chuck Band, owner of Cherry Creek Coin, assured him it would be no problem. The man thanked him and left, promising to return after closing the real estate deal. The entire conversation lasted less than ten minutes. Chuck didn't give it a second thought.

The man visited several other Denver coin dealers that same day. He asked the same questions about gold bullion coins, thanked them, and left. None of the other dealers gave it a second thought either.

True to his word, the would-be investor returned to Cherry Creek Coin a couple of weeks later on a Friday morning.

"Remember me?" he asked. "I'm the guy who wanted to invest fifteen thousand dollars in bullion coins."

"I remember," Chuck replied. "Have a seat. I'll see what I have in the safe."

Returning with coins in hand, Chuck said, "I'm a little short today. I've only got about ten thousand worth on hand."

"It's a beginning. Say, I hope you can take cashier's check," the visitor said, pulling one from inside his sports jacket. "I've just come from the real estate closing. The check's for fifteen thousand. I'd hoped you'd have that much in bullion coins."

Chuck frowned. He wasn't in the habit of taking large checks from strangers.

"I just closed the deal this morning," the visitor explained. "Drove directly over from Grand Junction. I assumed a bank check would be okay."

Chuck looked at the cashier's check. It was drawn on the Exchange Bank of Grand Junction. "I'll have to verify it with the bank," he said.

"Go right ahead."

Chuck reached information, requested the number of the Exchange Bank of Grand Junction, jotted it down, then called the bank.

"Exchange Bank, may I help you?" a pleasant female voice asked.

"I'd like to verify a cashier's check drawn on your bank," Chuck said.

"I can do that for you."

"It's made out to Mr. Ewing Larson."

"Just a moment, please."

Check in hand while he waited, Chuck studied the man seated across from him. He was in his early forties, average build, dressed in a beige sweater and sports jacket. Soft-spoken and pleasant, he wore a neatly trimmed brown beard. He reminded Chuck of a college professor.

"Yes, we issued the check," the female voice said, coming back on the line. "It's perfectly good."

"Thank you," Chuck said, then hung up.

"Everything all right?" the visitor asked.

"No problem. The check's good. The gold comes to $9,945. I can send you the rest of the coins in few days. I'm expecting more early next week." Handing the check back to Larson, he said, "Just endorse the back, and I'll get your receipt."

A few moments later, Larson walked out the door and down the street to his car. He'd taken the precaution of parking a block away to foil any sharp-eyed employee's attempt to jot down his license number. He got in his car and drove away.

Ewing Larson—or whatever his name was—made the rounds of the other Denver coin dealers that morning. At each, he presented a cashier's check for $15,000 drawn on the Exchange Bank of Grand Junction. Each dealer verified the check. And at each, Larson walked out with gold coins in hand. By day's end, Ewing Larson had vanished with more than $100,000 in highly liquid, untraceable gold coins.

Early the following week, Chuck Band got the bad news from his bank. There was no ABA (American Banking Association) routing number on the cashier's check nor could they find a listing for the Exchange Bank of Grand Junction in the ABA directory. Without an ABA number, there was no way to process the check.

The reason they couldn't find an ABA number in the ABA directory was because the Exchange Bank of Grand Junction didn't exist. The check was no good, a complete phony. The coin dealers had been cleverly hoaxed.

The scam was based on one simple, yet absolutely brilliant, element: bank verification of the bogus cashier's checks.

Weeks earlier, the con man had arrived in Grand Junction, rented a storefront in a new shopette, paid a deposit and a month's rent. He ordered telephone service installed in the storefront under the fictitious name, Exchange Bank of Grand Junction. He told the telephone company that the storefront was a temporary location while arrangements were being made for the new bank's permanent site. The phone company accepted the order at face value and installed the phone. The new number was entered in the phone company's database under the name Exchange Bank of Grand Junction. There it waited, ready for anyone who asked for it.

Next the con man cased Denver coin dealers to learn who kept sufficient gold on hand to make a worthwhile target. Printing the phony cashier's checks was the simplest part of the scheme.

On D-day, with his female accomplice standing by the phone at the nonexistent Exchange Bank of Grand Junction, he struck. The coin dealers acted predictably. Each called to verify the cashier's check, and each was completely taken in by the reassuring voice on the other end of the line.

By the time the scam was discovered, the con man and his accomplice were thousands of miles away, no doubt setting up another phony Exchange Bank. As far as I know, they've never been caught.

While on the subject of phony cashier's checks, a last anecdote. Another enterprising con man bought a legitimate cashier's check for $5,000 from a large, well-known Denver bank, then expertly reproduced several copies, all indistinguishable from the original. He, too, made the rounds of Denver coin dealers, buying bullion coins. Predictably, each dealer called the bank to verify the check. The name of the payee, date, check's serial number, every detail agreed with the bank's record of the genuinely issued check. In each case, the con artist walked out with gold in hand. You can imagine the coin dealers' surprise and outrage when the checks bounced, and they learned they had been victimized by yet another flim-flam man.

LIVE AND LET DIE

September 1975 was a long time ago, but I remember it like yesterday. In those days, I'd drop in about once a week on Russ Spalding, who owned Downtown Stamp & Coin in Englewood, Colorado. We'd trade gossip, see what we could buy from one another, talk about what deals were in the wind, then have lunch at our favorite diner, Cafe Ensenada.

I'd arrive about eleven-thirty. By noon, Russ's teenage helper, Ray, would waltz through the front door, then Russ and I would be off to lunch.

Downtown Stamp & Coin was an old-fashioned street-front stamp-and-coin store. It was narrow inside, and deep. Display cases ran the length of the store, forming a right angle at the rear. The cases toward the front displayed stamps; those toward the rear, coins. Half a dozen tall stools provided seating for customers.

Russ was a straightforward, unpretentious guy, and Downtown Stamp & Coin was a meat and potatoes place—no champagne or caviar. I remember arriving one morning just in time to see two flannel-shirted, Levi-clad men—one younger, one middle-aged—lugging white canvas bags out the front door to a waiting, mud-spattered pickup truck that looked like something out of the Grapes of Wrath. A third young man waited in the front seat of the truck, pump shotgun in hand.

"Farmer and his boys putting away a couple bags of survival silver," Russ explained. "They don't trust banks. Come in a couple times a year. Always park right out front. One son stays in the truck with a shotgun. The old man never says much. I have no idea what his name is. Always pays cash. Then they lug the bags out, warily as if they expect trouble, hoist them into the back of the truck, and off they go. They've got to be from out east, Bennett or Strasburg or Limon," he said, referring to small towns on the eastern high plains of Colorado.

I always enjoyed wheeling and dealing with Russ. He drove a hard bargain but was scrupulously fair and absolutely true to his word. And I looked forward to our weekly lunch breaks at Cafe Ensenada.

Elena Santiago owned and operated Cafe Ensenada, which boasted the best homemade Mexican food in town. Elena's green chile, smooth as Thanksgiving gravy yet fiery as a fiesta pinwheel, remains unsurpassed in my experience. A platter of Elena's green chile burritos and a tall, cold bottle of Superior, a smooth Mexican beer, were just about as close to heaven as you could get in downtown Englewood.

I had nothing more on my mind than some good-natured haggling and a plate of Elena's delicious burritos when I walked into Downtown Stamp & Coin that fateful morning in September 1975. Trouble was the last thing I expected.

Russ and I didn't do much business that morning. We just passed the time waiting for Ray. At about a quarter to noon, the phone rang. It was a longish call. Russ didn't do much talking, mostly listened. Occasionally, he muttered and jotted. "Mmm-hmm." Pause, jot. "A woman?" Pause, jot. "Mmm-hmm. What was she wearing?" Pause, jot. "What year was it? Mmm-hmm. I sure will. I'll let you know if I see it."

When he finished, he banged the phone down, ripped a sheet of paper from the note pad, and moved up toward the front of the store where I was waiting.

"Dennis With over at Collectors Coin Exchange just got ripped off!" he exclaimed.

Collectors Coin Exchange catered to an upscale clientele. It had the ambiance of a Rodeo Drive jewelry store: elegant, fashionable, plush furnishings, and a staff in three-piece suits.

"A girl walked in dressed in red, wearing running shoes. She looked like she was in her early twenties. She asked to see several rare coins from a velvet display tray under the glass counter. Dennis handed her one coin at a time. After she'd looked at three or four, she pointed to an especially expensive coin, a gem uncirculated 1907 ten-dollar gold piece, the Indian head variety with no motto. Dennis handed her the coin. She looked at it, then questioned the price, so Dennis turned around to get a copy of the Red Book to show her the listing. The instant he turned his back, she bolted. By the time he turned around with the book, she was on her way out the door. He raced around the counter, but she ran so fast he couldn't see where she'd gone by the time he reached the front door."

Collectors Coin Exchange was located on the second floor inside the sprawling Cinderella City shopping mall, which contained a maze of interconnected corridors housing hundreds of retail establishments. Even during the week, thousands of shoppers thronged its passageways.

"She got clean away, lost in the crowd," Russ said.

"What's a coin like that worth?" I asked.

"A few thousand bucks. It's pretty scarce, especially gem uncirculated. Dennis said he had ANACS papers on it." The ANACS (American Numismatic Association Certification Service) certificate contained a photo of the coin.

Stolen coins, as well as stolen stamps, often just disappear, usually taken out of state and sold. We assumed that the coin was history, the issued closed.

Russ couldn't have been off the phone more than ten minutes, when, just before noon, a young man in his early twenties nonchalantly strode in. He was cheerful, easygoing, and self-confident, the kind of guy who, after ten minutes' conversation, you feel you've known for years.

"Hi. What can I do for you?" Russ asked, walking toward the front of the store to meet him.

I was seated on one of the tall stools on the customer side of the counter, marking time until Ray showed up.

"I've got a coin I'd like to sell," he said. "My uncle in Iowa died recently and left it to me." He plopped a shiny ten-dollar gold piece mounted in a clear plastic holder on the counter.

Instantly, both Russ and I recognized it as Dennis With's stolen coin. My mind raced. Should I tackle the thief? I was on the same side of the counter. I was confident I could take him down. But was he armed? Would Russ try to call the police? Should I leave and try to alert the police?

I decided to sit tight and follow Russ's lead.

Russ didn't act surprised, nor did he give the slightest hint that he wanted me to do anything. In fact, he reacted rather coolly, didn't bat an eye as he picked up the coin.

"Very nice," he said, thoughtfully turning it over and over. "Beautiful coin."

"Yeah, my uncle was a *real* collector . . . just loved coins. There are a lot more in the collection, but this is the only one I want to sell right now."

"You've got a gorgeous piece here," Russ said, looking up from the coin. "It's worth a lot of money."

"Just how much?" the thief asked, elbows on the counter, relaxed and at ease.

"Several thousand dollars. It's a gem, but I don't get much call for high-powered material. If I bought it, I'd probably have to sit on it for a long time, and I can't afford to do that."

"Look, I don't expect to get full retail. I know you've got to make a profit. Make me an offer."

"I don't want to insult you," Russ started to say. Then, "Say, I've got an idea," he blurted out, looking at his wristwatch. "I've got a customer who just might be interested in this coin. If I call him right now, maybe he can come over during lunch hour and look at it. If he likes it, he'll buy it on the spot. Pay full retail. And I'd only have to make ten percent on the deal. Fair enough?"

"Sounds great. Let's do it!" the thief said.

Russ glanced at his watch again as he turned for the phone. "I hope he hasn't left for lunch yet." He punched up the number.

"Dennis With, please. This is Russ at Downtown Stamp & Coin." Turning to the thief and winking, he said, "I think we're in luck."

When Dennis With came on the line, Russ said, "I've got a coin I think you'd like to see. It's a beauty, a gem uncirculated 1907 ten-dollar Indian head with no motto. The seller's here now. I thought you might like to come over and look at it."

Russ put his hand over the receiver and said to the thief, "He's very interested. Says he can be here in ten or fifteen minutes. Is that okay?"

"No problem. Tell him to come ahead."

"He'll be waiting," Russ said into the mouthpiece. "See you shortly."

Russ hung up. Now, it was just a matter of waiting to see what would happen.

"This guy's a real high roller," Russ said, chatting up the thief. "If he likes it, he'll write a check on the spot."

"That's great, but I'll need cash, no checks. I'm moving to L.A. from Iowa. I don't have a checking account yet, so it's gotta be cash. In fact, if I didn't need the cash, I wouldn't be selling Uncle Willie's coin."

"Don't worry. The man's check is as good as gold. My bank's only a couple of blocks away. I can cash it for you. No problem."

The thief seemed satisfied. Meanwhile, Russ kept up a patter of small talk. "Whereabouts in Iowa did your uncle live?"

"Davenport. He was into farming. Owned a section there."

I listened, sure the thief was just making things up as he went along.

"You going into farming, too?" Russ asked, feigning interest.

"Nah, his son's going to get it."

I wondered why the son wasn't getting the coins too, but decided that things really don't have to make sense in an invented story.

The thief looked at his watch. The minutes dragged by.

"My guy's into oil," Russ said. You've probably heard of him— Withco Exploration. Hottest oil company around. Making money hand over fist. Got his own private jet and limos. Flies all over the world making deals. Hey, a few grand's nothing to him." The thief listened to Russ's distracting patter. And, for his part, Russ seemed to be enjoying the charade.

"Of course, we've been friends for years. I met him long before he made it big. That's why I know he's gonna love the coin."

"Let's hope so," the thief said, again glancing at his watch. It had been only a few minutes since he'd come in, but it felt like an eternity.

Finally, a tall man in a well-tailored business suit walked briskly in and strode purposefully over to the counter. A shorter, stockier man, whose sports coat and slacks seemed vaguely out of sync, lingered near the front door.

"Here's the coin," Russ said. Dennis With looked it over quickly—first, one side; then, the other. He turned to the shorter man and said, "This is the coin."

The shorter man advanced toward the thief. "Englewood Police," he said, brushing back his sports coat to reveal a holstered pistol. He continued forward but made no move to draw the weapon. Again, I wondered if the thief was armed and how he'd react. Dennis and the police officer were between him and the front door. He'd have to go through Russ and me to get out the back.

"Keep your hands on the counter," the officer warned, "and don't move." A moment later two more police officers rushed through the front door, and it was all over.

"Hey, what's going on here?" the thief demanded.

"This is my coin," With snarled, waving the coin in the thief's face, "Your thieving girlfriend stole it."

"You don't know what you're talking about. I got that coin from my uncle in Iowa."

"Can you prove that coin's yours?" the detective asked.

"Damn right," With retorted angrily. "I got an ANACS photo certificate for it right here." He pulled the certificate from his suit pocket and handed it to the detective. "No two coins are one hundred percent alike. Look at the photo. See how the distinguishing marks on the photo exactly match those on this coin."

The detective was satisfied. He turned to the thief and said, "What do you have to say to that?" The man merely shrugged. "Where's your girlfriend?" Silence. "Okay, you're under arrest. Put your hands on the wall."

As he turned to face the wall, the thief looked at me for an instant, a smug, self-confident smirk on his face. He wasn't the slightest bit upset. It wasn't at all the reaction I expected. I expected him to struggle, or make a break, or something. I guess I expected more excitement. Instead, he ceased his protests of innocence and submitted calmly to arrest. Suddenly, I realized he'd been through it all before. He was a pro, and it was a game to him.

The detective patted him down and snapped on handcuffs. While the drama played itself out, I stood not ten feet away. I studied the thief with the same intrigued curiosity that a biologist might display toward a new species he'd just seen for the first time. I'd never been face to face with an apprehended criminal.

The thing I remember most distinctly about that morning is the arrogant aloofness of the man, his self-assured, uncaring smirk.

The arrest took only a few minutes. As they marched the suspect out the door, Ray walked in. "Hey, what's all the excitement?" he said.

"We just nailed a crook," Russ replied. And with that, we adjourned to Cafe Ensenada to celebrate.

Later that day, they apprehended the female accomplice. The pair was arraigned, then released on their own recognizance. Trial was scheduled for October 23, 1975. The District Attorney subpoenaed Russ to testify at the trial.

On October 24, Russ and I met for our weekly lunch at Cafe Ensenada.

"How'd the trial go?" I asked.

"There wasn't any. They didn't show. They skipped out."

"You'd think that for a major theft they'd at least make the guy post bail. What happens now?"

"The judge put out a bench warrant for them, but a lot of good that'll do. They're long gone."

I remembered the thief's smirk. I wasn't a criminologist, but even I could see that being arrested hadn't bothered him in the slightest. He was obviously experienced. Why would they release him without a sizable bond? I didn't know.

"At least, Dennis will get his coin back," I said.

"Yeah, they released it to him. I guess it's their way of saying, 'We're not going to catch the guy, so why bother to keep the evidence?' "

Russ was right, and that seemed to be the end of it.

But it wasn't.

A few weeks later, in early November, again over a plate of Elena's delicious green chile burritos, Russ said, "Remember Bonnie and Clyde?" Bonnie and Clyde were Russ's nicknames for the pair of thieves.

"Sure."

"Well, they're back in the news again." He handed me a page from *The Denver Post*. The headline read, "Pair Held in Baby-Death Probe." I scanned the article.

Nevada authorities were continuing Wednesday to hold a Denver man and his wife in connection with the death of their 6-month-old son who weighed only three pounds.

Sheriff Pete Rasner of Carson City, Nevada, said a preliminary report from a pathologist showed the baby weighed only three pounds at death and there were no signs of food in the baby's stomach.

The preliminary pathology report also showed the baby had fractures of the head and face and was suffering from pneumonia, rickets, malnutrition and hepatitis, Rasner said.

The baby was in a car bed in the car and had been dead for twelve hours, the sheriff said.

Although the temperature had dropped to twelve degrees that night, he said, the baby was covered with only a light blanket and wasn't wearing a diaper, shirt or any other clothing.

He said the parents reportedly were across the street in a gambling casino during the night.

He said a routine check showed the pair were wanted on an Arapahoe County [Colorado] warrant accusing them of theft and theft by receiving and also are suspects in a burglary at Virginia City, Nevada.

According to Arapahoe County authorities, the pair was arrested early in September in connection with the theft of a coin from an Englewood coin shop and released on personal recognizance. A bench warrant was issued for their arrest when they failed to appear in court October 23, they said.

I put the paper down and looked up at Russ.

"Nice couple, huh?" Russ said.

Suddenly, I didn't feel like eating. The thief's arrogant smirk flashed into memory. It was the single indelible characteristic that overshadowed every other feature of the man; it seemed to sum him up. I could see that terrible, haunting smile as clearly as if it were yesterday, as clearly as if he were sitting across the table from me. It was chilling and grotesque, and I'll never forget it as long as I live.

Months passed and the episode faded. Dozens of lunches later, the tragedy finally reached its conclusion.

"I just found out what happened to Bonnie and Clyde," Russ said. "They're serving life in Nevada for murder. Colorado's got a request for extradition on the theft charge, but that will have to wait until the Nevada sentence is served."

"Well, it looks like you won't be testifying anytime soon," I said.

"You know what," Russ said, grimacing as he bit into the slice of lime from the rim of his tall glass of Superior, "I've often wondered what would've happened if they'd been kept in jail on the theft charge and not been able to skip out."

"I guess we'll never know," I sighed, still profoundly mystified about how a mother could let her infant child freeze to death while she reveled and gambled the night away. "I guess we'll never know."

A TICKET TO RIDE

On Saturday afternoon, March 11, 1989, Henry Pobuda strolled into J.B. Peterson's Stamps and Coins on East Colfax in Aurora, Colorado. He walked down the long narrow entryway, past the display cases, to the chair-lined counter where a Saturday afternoon crowd intently pored over plump counterbooks and boxes stuffed with covers. He set his attaché case on an empty chair to reserve it. Then he headed to the rear of the store to check out new arrivals on the shelves that housed the large lots, collections and accumulations.

Henry's attaché case contained three Scott No. C18 first day covers, a stock book of nineteenth century U.S. stamps cataloging $5,000, and more than a hundred other covers with an aggregate value of several hundred dollars.

The ambiance at Peterson's was informal, like a big, warm, old-fashioned country store. To Jim Peterson, who owned and operated the store, it made no difference whether you were a ten-year-old making a fifty-cent purchase or a veteran collector buying a set of Zeppelins. Both received the same patient, courteous treatment. Peterson's motto was: "Something for every collector." And was true. Peterson's boasted Denver's largest inventory of stamps, a rich and varied stock built up over decades. It was a popular place to socialize with philatelic friends and see lots of stamps. Henry, like everyone active in philately in Denver, had been there countless times and spent countless hours enjoying the ambiance and the stamps.

Henry didn't think twice about leaving his attaché case on the chair. He'd done it many times before. He busied himself with the pleasant task of searching remainders and boxes of covers for anything promising. Occasionally, he glanced at the chair to check on his attaché case, not because he was worried, but from habit. Suddenly, an item in one of the boxes caught his attention. He thought it might be a Scott No. 540 on cover. He scrutinized it for a long, distracting moment. Yes, he decided, it is a No. 540. Then, when he looked up again to check his attaché case, the chair was empty. The attaché case was gone.

On that same Saturday afternoon, at the same time Henry Pobuda's attaché case disappeared, I was busy catering to customers at my booth at WESTEX, which was being held at the John Q. Hammons Trade Center located a couple of miles north of J.B. Peterson's. The WESTEX bourse was large; the sprawling trade center accommodated well over a hundred stamp and coin dealers. Stamp dealers were grouped together at one end of the hall, coins dealers at the other end. My table was located against the far wall, giving me an excellent view of the entire show.

In stark contrast to his usual cheerful, good-natured air, Henry Pobuda looked pale and troubled as he approached my booth.

"Steve, I've been ripped off!" he said. "It happened about an hour ago over at Jim Peterson's. I thought I'd better get over here and spread the word, on the outside chance the slimeball shows up and tries to unload the stamps."

"How'd it happen?" I asked. "What's missing?"

"I set the case on a chair to reserve it and went back to look at the new large lots. A guy just picked it up and walked out with it. I got preoccupied because I thought I'd found a pretty good stamp on cover. When I looked up, the case was gone. I had three baby Zepp covers in it, a stock book with about five thousand bucks in nineteenth century material, and a hundred to a hundred and fifty covers, FDCs, etc. It's my own fault. I shouldn't have left it alone. It was there one minute, gone the next."

Henry's news startled me. Stamp collectors are a pretty honest bunch. I couldn't imagine who would steal Henry's attaché case.

"Do you know who did it?" I asked.

"I've got a description of the guy, but I don't know his name. When I realized the case was missing, I ran out the front door to see if I could catch whoever snatched it. On the way out, I brushed past

Alex Ionnides, who was just coming in. 'Hey, what's the big hurry?' he asked, but I didn't have time to answer. I wanted to nail the guy. I was out the door in a flash. I looked up and down the street, but he was gone.

"I went back in to call the cops, and, again, Alex asked what happened. When I told him, he blurted out, 'Why didn't you say something? I just passed a guy with an attaché case on my way in. He was coming around the side of the building. It's gotta be the same guy! He did look kind of suspicious. When you ran out, you must have missed him by only a few seconds.'

"I called the police," Henry said. "They made a report and put out an APB based on Alex's description: black male, about six feet two, wearing a black shirt, black pants, and black jacket.

"It's my own fault, Steve. I shouldn't have left the case alone, even for a moment. I was careless, but I never expected anyone to walk off with it, especially in front of all those people."

Having been ripped off myself, I knew exactly how Henry felt: white-hot anger; kicking yourself for having been careless; anxiety over the loss; utter hopelessness in knowing that you'll probably never see your stamps again, and perhaps worst of all, knowing there's nothing you can do about it.

"They ought to lock the son of a bitch up and throw away the key," Henry rumbled, punctuating the remark with a grimace. "Instead, he'll probably get a fifty-dollar fine—suspended—and ten hours of community service—*if* they catch him, which they probably won't."

Henry's reaction reflected his frustration. He knew there was little likelihood the guy would be caught or that he'd ever see his stamps again.

"I'll keep my eyes open," I said. "Maybe he'll show up here and we can nab him."

"Thanks, but I doubt he'd be that stupid. I'll cover the bases anyway, just in case. I'd better let the other guys know," Henry said, moving on. During the next few minutes, Henry made his way from booth to booth, re-telling his story. I sympathized with him. At least, being among friends provided moral support.

When he had finished alerting the dealers, Henry headed for the restroom in the hallway outside the show. At nearly the same moment, Randy Groves walked into WESTEX. Henry Pobuda missed him by only a few seconds.

Groves' first stop was Max Hickox's bourse table. Max immediately recognized him from Henry's description and sent him to Joe & Val's Stamps. Joe & Val's table was located in the corner most distant from the door. Max reasoned that it would be more difficult for Groves to escape from the rear of the hall, should he decide to flee. As Groves made his way to Joe & Val's, Randy Nilson, another bourse dealer, realized who he was and hurried to the lobby to alert security.

At Joe & Val's Stamps, operated by Joe Neri and Val McDaniel, Groves asked Joe if he would be interested in buying the stock book of nineteenth century U.S. stamps. The asking price: $500. Joe began to flip through the stock book. Then, turning his back to Groves as if to consult with his partner Val, he whispered, "These are Henry's stolen stamps."

Neither Joe nor Val were aware that Groves had stopped at Hickox's table. Nor were they aware that Randy Nilson had gone to alert security. So they quickly formulated their own plan. Joe would try to stall Groves; Val would attempt to alert security. Joe paged through the stock book slowly, like a snail on his way home after a hard day at work.

Val decided not to leave the booth. He didn't want to make Groves suspicious. Instead, he moved to the far corner of their double booth and attempted to unobtrusively signal security. Val worried that Groves might be armed, that he might use a weapon if challenged or cornered. The show was crowded with people, and Val was concerned that someone might be hurt or killed if a violent confrontation developed. So, unaware that security had been alerted, he signaled as frantically as he could, trying not to be too obvious, hoping someone would see him.

Meanwhile, when Randy Nilson reached the lobby, he ran into Henry as Henry emerged from the restroom. Together, they alerted show security—uniformed, off-duty Aurora police officers. The police instructed Henry to go to Joe and Val's booth and make sure the stamps were his. They would cover the exits while Henry made his verification.

"Can I see that book?" Henry asked a surprised Randy Groves. Groves froze. Peterson's had been crowded, and the attaché case unattended, so Groves had no way of knowing that Henry was its owner. But he seemed to recognize Henry as one of the customers who had been in Peterson's, and it made him uneasy. He began to tremble and pace nervously, as Henry examined the book. After a quick glance, he handed it back to Groves, then turned and headed for the door, signaling police as he went.

About that time, I glanced up from my busy table and saw Henry headed toward the lobby. I also saw Groves at Joe and Val's and realized that he must be the thief. I could see Joe talking to him, but I couldn't hear what was being said. I wondered what to do. Questions raced through my head: What was going on at Joe and Val's table? Was the man armed? What would happen if he broke and ran? How could I help? The scene seemed to play out in slow motion.

Joe continued to stall, perusing the stock book slowly, carefully. Groves, increasingly jumpy, whined insistently, "C'mon man, what's the problem?"

"I can't give five hundred," Joe replied. "I've only got a hundred seventy in cash." Groves was clearly spooked. He wanted out immediately.

"Okay, okay, gimme the one seventy." Even if Joe had been unaware of the theft, he would have known something was wrong. A legitimate collector doesn't ask $500 for a stock book containing $5,000 catalogue value in better U.S., then, without argument, settle for a mere $170. Joe gave Groves the money in order to secure Henry's stamps. He was afraid that if Groves somehow escaped with the stock book, Henry would never see his stamps again.

Groves grabbed the $170 and made for a side exit. Once through the door, he started down the hallway leading away from the lobby and to a building exit.

"Hey, you!" a voice boomed. "Hold it right there!" Groves froze in his tracks. "I want to talk to you," a uniformed officer said, closing in on him. Groves offered no resistance. They stood him up against the wall, patted him down, then handcuffed him. They found no weapons on him, but they did find some of Henry's covers.

"Hey, can't you cut me some slack?" Groves whined. "This is the first time I've been in any trouble." He trembled with fear. "Cut me a break, man. I'll never do anything like this again, I swear." Groves looked pathetic, hands cuffed behind his back, face to the wall, quavering. Henry, on the other hand, was jubilant.

Groves didn't stand trial for the theft of Henry Pobuda's stamps. On April 13, 1990, as the result of a plea bargain agreement, he was sentenced to 90 days in jail and two years probation. He served a few weeks in jail, then, due to jail overcrowding; he was released on home detention. On July 8, 1990, his "jail time" completed, he began his two years probation.

As part of the plea bargain, Groves was ordered to make restitution for Henry's attaché case and those covers not recovered at the time of his arrest. Groves had maintained that he didn't know where Henry's other covers were. But on the day of sentencing, rather than pay restitution in cash, Groves suddenly produced the missing covers.

Now, a couple of items just to wrap things up. Randy Groves lied. He had had several prior arrests. He was an experienced felon. And Henry Pobuda, although unaware of it at the time, had laid the groundwork for Groves' capture. On the afternoon of the theft, he had planned to attend WESTEX after visiting Peterson's. In his attaché case, right on top of all the stamps and covers, where Groves couldn't possibly miss them, he'd placed a complimentary ticket to WESTEX and a publicity map showing how to get there. Fortunately for Henry Pobuda, Groves took advantage of the free ticket and the map.

GONE WITHOUT A TRACE

The rolling farmlands that abut the foothills of the Rockies in northern Colorado are wonderfully green and lush with corn, wheat and sugar beets in summer. By October, they've become brown stubble-fields, dotted with foraging Canada geese newly arrived from the high Arctic. Canada geese have a great advantage over humans; they can fly above the checkerboard landscape and go directly to their destinations. I wasn't so lucky. I had to weave my way through a maze of unpaved back roads to find the Marsh residence.

Mrs. Marsh lived way out in the country at the kind of address you find by going three miles beyond the Texaco station to the junction, then left until you reach County Road 19, then about two miles until you come to a "T" in the road, then right about a mile or so until you pass a small lake, then you watch for a red brick house on the left. The name "Marsh" is on the mailbox. The invariable, encouraging final comment is, "You can't miss it!"

Mrs. Marsh's adult daughter, Sandra Owens, greeted me at the front door when I arrived. "Come right in," she said, holding the screen door wide for me.

I stepped into a typical farm home. It was a lived-in place, clean, comfortable, and well organized, although it gave the impression of being somewhat cluttered. I've often wondered if farm homes are furnished according to some secret protocol. It seems they're nearly always filled to overflowing with strikingly similar things such as feedstore calendars, jars of colored corn and bean seed, gnarled pieces of driftwood, old spinning wheels, cast-iron gadgets whose purpose has long since been forgotten, mock-silk, fringed, commemorative pillows inscribed "Grand Canyon 1934" or "Niagara Falls 1938," crocheted comforters, and raggedy dolls and china dolls clad in bright calico dresses.

"Come right in," Sandra said, ushering me into the kitchen. "Make yourself at home."

The kitchen is the heart of a farm home, the room where things get done. On the Marsh's kitchen table lay several fat Minkus international albums. A dozen or so oversized three-ring binders were piled next to it. The balance—packets, bags of kiloware, loose stamps, catalogues, and the usual miscellany—filled several large cardboard cartons on the floor next to the table.

"Mother is elderly and spends most of the day in bed," Sandra informed me. "Dad's been gone seven years now, and those years have been rough on her."

I took a seat at the kitchen table and listened politely. I didn't open any of the albums, considering it rude to do so before Sandra finished speaking—like beginning to eat before your host has finished saying grace. Conversation breaks the ice or, perhaps, satisfies the unconscious need of the seller to explain why the collection is on the market.

"Actually, it's been hard on all of us," she continued, "but at least now we can try to get his things in order."

I wondered why they had waited so many years to sell the collection.

"Dad loved his stamps and his rocks. Spent hours and hours working with the albums, writing to other collectors, trading with them. He wanted to see how many stamps he could accumulate without spending any money on them. He was pretty emphatic about it, too. 'The challenge is trying to build the largest collection possible without spending any money,' he liked to say. He felt that money somehow tainted the purity of any hobby."

My heart sank. Glancing at the plump albums and boxes, I knew I was on another wild-goose chase. It wasn't necessary to open an album; I knew what I'd find. Sandra's revealing remark, "build the largest collection possible without spending any money," had said it all.

"Let me take a quick look and see what we've got here," I suggested. Knowing the collection wasn't going to amount to much, I wanted to get started, finish up, and be on my way. One after another, the albums confirmed what I suspected. Mr. Marsh had corresponded and traded with a great many collectors. He had accumulated thousands and thousands of stamps. Unfortunately, they were ultra-common and generally in poor condition.

Mr. Marsh's approach to soaking stamps and preparing them for mounting was sloppy. One should never soak stamps on red paper, especially in warm water. By the look of it, Mr. Marsh made that mistake again and again. He must have bulk soaked, leaving stamps and red paper in water too long. Numerous examples of this careless procedure dotted page after album page like a rash. They ranged in hue from slightly pinkish at best, to beet red at worst. Pink is a wonderful color on flamingos, peach blossoms, and rare steaks, but not on stamps. Even the key items—such as they were—suffered. A once proud $5 Coolidge bearing a magenta oval cancel was disfigured by an ugly, ruby-colored bleed. A $1 Airlift blushed, tinted the hue of a freshly boiled lobster.

Nor had Mr. Marsh mastered the art of drying and pressing stamps. Rather than being smooth, they were warped and gave the album pages an uneven, rumpled appearance. They crackled when turned. He must have soaked stamps en masse, drying them on layers of newsprint without sufficient weight to press them completely flat. Or perhaps he removed them before they were completely dry. Whatever the reason, the result was unsightly.

Mr. Marsh hadn't been selective. No, that's too diplomatic. Mr. Marsh had been oblivious to the concept of condition. Damaged stamps abounded, even stamps with pieces missing. As long as it filled a space, it was okay. So zealous had Mr. Marsh been in his quest to avoid spending money, that every last stamp in the collection was cancelled—every single, solitary stamp. There wasn't a mint stamp in the bunch, not even a lowly one-cent definitive.

He had separated foreign stamps into country groupings, but within a grouping, stamps were hodgepodged together with no apparent rhyme or reason. The result of this effort—the voluminous correspondence, the energetic trading, the careless soaking, the indiscriminate mounting—was a big mess.

Coincidentally, a year before, I had been invited to make an offer on a similar collection at a farm couple's home located only about twenty miles away from the Marsh home. There, too, I had worked at a kitchen table, looked at an assemblage of ultra-common stamps hodgepodged on manila stock sheets in dime-store binders. When I asked the farmer what he wanted for the collection, he replied in all seriousness, "Fifty thousand dollars." The figure was so absurd I could only conclude that either he was crazy or thought I was a fool.

"How did you arrive at fifty thousand dollars?" I asked him.

"Well, there's at least fifty thousand stamps here, and I figured they ought to be worth at least a buck apiece."

"They're not worth a buck a hundred, let alone a buck apiece," I replied. It wasn't a counteroffer, which would have been pointless. Still, I reasoned, someone ought to shine a little daylight into his dark closet.

"That's okay," he said, completely unperturbed. "I'll just hang onto 'em until they are."

Back at the Marsh home, Sandra busied herself with household chores while I looked over her father's collection. The inspection didn't take long. There were no stamps of significant value. But then, after Sandra's remark about her father's philosophy on collecting, I didn't expect to find any.

"I'm finished," I announced the next time she came into the kitchen.

"That was fast," she replied.

"Well, it was pretty routine. What you've got here is a massive accumulation of very common stamps, the kind you figure by the pound or by the thousand. They have little individual value. You said your father wanted to see how many stamps he could accumulate without spending any money, and I'm afraid the result reflects that."

"I guess I shouldn't be too surprised. How much is it worth?"

"Based on bulk, perhaps a couple of hundred dollars."

"That's not very much."

"True, but the stamps are ultra-common. It won't bother me a bit if you decide to keep the collection. Its sentimental value no doubt exceeds its market value. It's the kind of collection that retails for fifteen or twenty dollars an album—again, based on nothing more than sheer bulk. It's not the kind of collection that you break up. Too much labor, too little profit. Frankly, it's not the kind of collection I normally make an offer on, but since I'm already here, I'll take it if you'd rather not keep it."

"I'll have to check with Mom. Say, do you know anything about rocks and minerals?"

"Not really," I said.

"Dad's real passion was rocks and minerals. He was a real rockhound. He's got thousands of specimens. Let me show you." She led me to a small den off the kitchen.

Shelves loaded with rocks lined the walls. Half a dozen glass-doored cabinets crowded with specimens stood like museum displays. Larger specimens, some the size of basketballs, cluttered the floor. Every square inch of this cross between a museum and a cave was filled with rocks—big rocks, little rocks, crystals, flints, geodes, marble, obsidian, gold ore, turquoise, and hundreds of others I couldn't even begin to guess at. To me, it looked like a genuine treasure-trove.

Would a mineral collector or dealer be as impressed as I was? Perhaps. But then someone knowledgeable in minerals might be overly impressed by the stamp collection, unaware of its commonness. Were the minerals as common as the stamps? I didn't know. Still, they made an impressive display.

"Dad was out looking for minerals the day he vanished," she said.

"Vanished?"

"Disappeared off the face of the earth . . . without a trace. He'd gone rock hunting with a friend of his, Gus—and not much a friend either, in my opinion. I think the only reason Gus hung around Dad was to take advantage of his knowledge of minerals and prospecting locations. I think he killed Dad, but I can't prove it."

"Surely you've told the police about your suspicions?"

"Oh, yes. The detective handling the case thought the circumstances surrounding Dad's death were unusual. He interviewed Gus several times, but Gus always stuck to his story. They'd gone prospecting in a remote area down by the Four Corners."

Arizona, Utah, New Mexico and Colorado meet at a common point known as the Four Corners.

"Gus claimed that after they arrived, he and Dad went their separate ways in search of specimens. Gus said he returned to the truck at about two o'clock, but Dad wasn't there. Dad's lunch hadn't been touched either. Gus assumed that Dad had gotten busy and decided to skip lunch. According to Gus, he waited until three o'clock, then went for help. He left the lunch and a note, weighted by a rock, explaining where he'd gone, in case Dad returned while he was away. But Dad never showed up, period.

"Dad was in his seventies. He couldn't stay out as many hours as he used to. He liked to start early, come back to his truck around noon for lunch, rest awhile, then spend another hour or two—maximum—tramping around.

"Anyway, the sheriff called out a search team. They spent the rest of the afternoon looking for Dad but didn't find much, except his hat. It was lying on the ground about a thousand feet from the point on the road where he and Gus had stopped. That's all they ever found.

"The more I thought about it," Sandra said, "the more the lack of clues struck me as unusual. A man leaves evidence that he's been somewhere—footprints, disturbed rocks, *something*. But other than the hat, they never found a thing. If Dad had had a stroke or heart attack, they would've found his body. A man just doesn't vanish off the face of the earth without a trace.

"And there's something else odd, too," Sandra said. "How did Gus get the keys to the truck to go for help?"

I listened, suddenly intrigued by the mystery.

"Gus claimed that Dad left the keys under the floor mat," Sandra said. "But I don't believe him. Dad wouldn't do that. He kept his keys in his pocket. It was a lifelong habit. He may have been a trusting soul, but he wasn't about to leave the keys to his new truck under the floor mat, especially out in the middle of nowhere. Dad loved that truck. It had four-wheel-drive and a winch on the front. He was enormously proud of it. Dad said it was probably the last new truck he'd ever own. No way would he go off and leave the keys to his pride and joy under the floor mat. *No way!*

"I think Gus killed Dad. I think he hit him over the head, then drove him out forty miles from nowhere and buried him. Gus had all morning. He could easily have driven anywhere off the main road with four-wheel-drive. He could've buried the body anywhere out there. That country's so remote the odds of anyone finding it are slim.

"After he disposed of the body, Gus drove back to the original prospecting site, spent a couple hours walking around, gathered a few samples to back up his story. He planted Dad's hat a thousand feet off the road in a convenient spot where the police were sure to find it."

"And the police believed his story?" I asked.

"I'm sure they did at first," Sandra said. "They had no reason to doubt him. They spent a couple of days looking for Dad. They figured he might have gotten disoriented, wandered off and gotten lost. They covered the immediate area with a thorough foot search. They used helicopters, mounted patrols, jeeps, the whole works for a broader search. But other than the hat, they never found a trace. It's as if he vanished into thin air."

Sandra's suspicions sounded reasonable to me.

"The police interviewed me several times," Sandra said. "I insisted that foul play was involved in Dad's disappearance, that Gus was almost certainly the culprit. Gus shouldn't have had the truck keys. They should've been on Dad. I told the detective that Dad would never leave his keys in the truck, that he kept them in his pocket—religiously. If Dad got lost, the keys should've been lost with him. I stressed that point again and again: *Dad would never leave his keys in an untended truck*. But the police weren't convinced.

"I told them they'd discover the truth if they'd just take the time to investigate Gus thoroughly. But it didn't do any good.

"At one point, I got to wondering if they thought I had an axe to grind with Gus, or if maybe I was just a troublemaker because I was so insistent. Perhaps I made too much of a pest of myself," she said, exhaling a deep sigh.

"I called the district attorney and demanded action. He pointed out that no body had ever been found, so there was no proof that a crime had been committed. They couldn't charge Gus or anyone else with murder without a body. All they had was a mysterious disappearance, and mysterious disappearance is not a crime. The DA said he had no tangible evidence that any crime had been committed. Suspicions, he said, weren't enough to arrest a man on.

"Then there's the question of motive. Gus seemed like a harmless fellow. 'Why would Gus want to kill your father?' the DA asked. I could only answer with suspicions.

"I think Gus was envious of Dad," Sandra said. "Perhaps Dad wouldn't take him to one of the places that he thought he ought to know about. Dad guarded his secrets closely. Perhaps they got into an argument. Perhaps Gus lost his temper and killed Dad in a rage. I don't know the whys or the hows, *but I am certain that Gus killed Dad.*

"Although Gus appeared harmless, he was strong as an ox . . . and about as bright. He was a big fellow, could have played a Neanderthal without much makeup. He was easygoing, but not talkative. He was so quiet, in fact, that you often wondered what was going on in his mind. Gus just wasn't right—nothing you could put your finger on. Even Dad used to say that he was three bricks short of a full load. He gave me the creeps.

"Then there's the possibility that Gus was after Dad's truck," Sandra said. "He came by shortly after Dad disappeared. I wasn't about to let him in the house, so we talked on the front porch. He asked what we were going to do with the new truck. I thought the question strange. I asked why he wanted to know. He said Dad once told him, that if anything ever happened to him, Gus could have the truck. Gus was pretty emphatic about it, too.

"I told Gus that we had decided to keep the truck so it would be here when Dad came returned. That surprised him, because he started to say something, then caught himself. He stood there for the longest time, just staring at me with that stone-blank face of his. I wondered what he'd been about to say . . . perhaps that Dad wouldn't be needing the truck? Finally, he said, 'Okay.' Then, turned and walked away. A shiver went down my spine as I watched him saunter out to the road. That encounter happened seven years ago, but I still get goosebumps whenever I think about it."

"And Gus has never been charged?" I asked.

"No."

"And your father has never been found?"

"No."

"And it's been seven years?"

"Yes, that's why I called you, because now we can sell the stamps. It's no picnic having someone disappear. It takes seven years for them to be declared legally dead. In the meantime, you're in limbo. You can't sell property, you can't settle affairs, all you can do is worry. And to make things worse, Dad never bothered to make a will. The whole thing's been a legal nightmare. Mom and Dad didn't have a lot of money. What little they did have is tied up in this place. Mom's not well, and she's been strapped for cash these last seven years. It's been hard. At least now we can start to get things settled."

Sandra Owens suddenly looked tired. "You might as well take the collection," she said. "It's one bit less clutter, and Mom can use the money. Our lawyer informed us last week that we could legally begin disposing of Dad's property.

"It's ironic, isn't it?" she said, fixing her eyes on me, thumping the open album on the table to emphasize her point. "You wait seven years to sell something, only to find out it isn't worth much.

"Go ahead, take it," she said. "I just want to get this whole affair behind me. Dad's never going to be found. Gus's never going to be charged. I realized that a long time ago . . . and I accept it." Her voice trailed off, as if finally suffocated by the weight of years of frustration. She had said what she had to say, not realizing at the beginning that recounting the ordeal of her father's disappearance would dispirit her so much.

I paid Sandra Owens $250 for her father's collection, loaded it into my car, and started home. On my left and only a few miles distant, massive Long's Peak jutted skyward, its snowy summit etched razor-sharp against a luminously blue Colorado sky. On my right, rolling, autumn-colored farmland stretched east to the horizon in giant, lazy, landlocked waves, like those in a Thomas Hart Benton landscape. Not the slightest wisp of a cloud marred the brilliant morning sky. The October air was like crystal—perfectly transparent, completely invisible. The miles-distant horizon remained in perfect focus, the most minute detail flawlessly defined.

I sped along the country roads, over hills that rose and fell like heavy seas, churning great clouds of khaki-colored dust in my wake. Somewhere to the south, near the Four Corners, under that same blindingly luminous azure sky, lay the answer to the mystery of Sandra Owens' father's disappearance. Something told me—that incredibly perfect fall morning—that it would remain a secret forever.

PART TWO

MISCHIEF & INTRIGUE

GOTCHA!

Stamp dealers love to tell deadbeat stories.

We've all been taken, and at the time of the loss it hurts and makes you mad as hell. Later, after the initial pain has subsided, the ingenuity of the clever chiseler can be more objectively appreciated. Some of their antics are downright funny. One of my favorites is a story related to me over lunch a few years back by Cliff Sutter, a dealer friend.

At the time, Cliff was experimenting with the approval business. He advertised in the classified section of philatelic periodicals to generate new leads and sold everything from inexpensive stamps to better issues.

Anyone who has ever entertained the notion of getting into the stamp business has probably considered selling approvals. The concept is simple. You send a selection of stamps to the customer. He looks them over for ten days, then returns the lot, remitting payment for those kept.

Unfortunately, in the approval business deadbeats are a fact of life. They won't put you out of business, but they *are* annoying. They order approvals, then don't pay for them, secure in the knowledge that there's little chance of being punished for ripping off a $10 or $20 selection. Nasty letters prompt a few to pay up, but mostly they ignore pleas and threats. They know there's no practical way for the dealer to force them to pay. Neither prosecutors nor collection agencies are willing to follow up such small cases.

To protect themselves from deadbeats, most approval dealers send new customers small selections with large markups. An initial $20 selection of colorful foreign topicals may cost as little as four or five dollars. More expensive, better stamps carry much smaller markups. They're sent later, after a customer has established his credit-worthiness.

"I got a letter requesting approvals from a man in Arizona," Cliff said. "He was building a U.S. collection. His return address was a post office box, which can be a red flag, so I sent him a small starter selection, eight or ten bucks worth. He bought the whole works, paid fast, and asked for another group. Paid for the second group just as fast and bought every stamp. His third selection was around thirty bucks. Again, he bought it all and paid promptly.

"I was impressed. He seemed like the ideal customer, the kind approval dealers love—takes the entire selection every time and pays fast. And I mean fast. He turned my letters around within a day or two of getting them. Wrote nice notes, too, complimenting me on the quality of the selections, my competitive prices, and good service. He said he was serious about building a quality U.S. collection—mint, never-hinged stamps in very fine or better condition—and looked forward to doing a lot of business with me in the years to come. He also asked if I serviced want lists. Sure, I told him. Just let me know what you need.

"His next letter requested about two hundred dollars' worth of medium priced stamps. He listed specific numbers, which I sent right away. He kept about a hundred seventy-five dollars' worth, returned the balance, and enclosed another wantlist. One look at the list and I knew he wasn't fooling around. He wanted mint Columbians, Trans-Mississippis, that sort of stuff, but only in top condition. So, I put together a gorgeous group—the best of what I had—and sent it off to him. It totaled about five hundred dollars."

Cliff paused to take another bite out of his sandwich. I knew what was coming. The deadbeat had set Cliff up for the big score.

"A couple of weeks went by and no reply," Cliff said. "I thought it was odd because the guy had been so prompt in the past. I assumed he was waiting until payday or until he could get the money together so he could buy the whole selection. After all, it was quite a lot larger than he had previously ordered. I wasn't really concerned at that point. He'd been so reliable in the past.

"Another week passed, and still no answer. So I jotted him a note to confirm that he'd received the stamps. It was possible that the shipment had been lost in the mail. If so, I was covered. I'd sent it by registered mail. I asked if there was a problem with payment. Did he need extra time? If so, okay. Given the size of the order, an extra week or two didn't bother me at all. I wanted to let him know I could be flexible, that I valued him as a customer.

"I figured I should hear from him within a week, judging from the speed of his earlier letters. But the week went by, and still no word. I began to get bad vibes. I sent another letter, certified mail, demanding immediate payment or the return of my stamps. It was the standard deadbeat first-warning letter. You know, pay up or your credit will be ruined.

"A few days later, a letter arrived with his return address on it," Cliff said. "I hoped it would contain a check and a note of explanation or apology. For all I knew, he might have been in an accident or laid up in the hospital for a couple of weeks. Stranger things have happened. Instead, it contained a note saying: 'Dear Cliff, I want you to know that you've been ripped by the best!'"

I laughed. Cliff, too, smiled.

"I can laugh now," he said. "But it wasn't too funny at the time. I was mad as hell!"

The deadbeat's sheer nerve, the way he so arrogantly flaunted his fraud in Cliff's face struck me as extraordinarily humorous.

"So, what did you do?" I asked.

"I wrote the S-O-B back and told him he wouldn't think it was too funny when I filed criminal mail fraud charges against him. Ripping off nickel-and-dime approval sets is one thing. Ripping off five hundred dollars' worth is a quite another. We're talking felony. I knew the Postal Service would take action with that amount of money involved. 'You've got three days to return my stamps or pay for them, or I'm filing criminal charges,' I threatened.

"I take it you didn't get your stamps back?"

"No. I got another letter. This guy was smooth. The letter said, 'Dear Cliff, I'm an inmate in the Arizona State Pen. I'm serving life for murder. Go ahead and sue me. File all the charges you want. What are they going to do? Give me another 20 years? Like I said, You've been ripped by the best. And there's not a damn thing you can do about it! *Ha-ha-ha!*'"

I laughed again, heartily. The humor was delicious, exquisite. Gambit, check, and checkmate.

"You wouldn't think it was so funny if it happened to you," Cliff protested.

"I'm sorry. It's just the unmitigated gall of the guy. Couldn't you complain to the warden? Get him locked up in solitary or something?" I asked.

"I wrote to the prison. There wasn't much they could do, or would do. They questioned the jerk. They searched his cell, but didn't find my stamps. They couldn't add time to his sentence without a trial. It was irrelevant, anyway. He was already serving life. Why waste money adding a few more years to the total? They guessed I could sue the man, but didn't think it would do much good. They couldn't arbitrarily seize the five bucks a week or whatever inmates get paid. They agreed to watch his mail, but a lot of good that's going to do me." Cliff finished his sandwich, took a leisurely swallow of iced tea, then said, "The guy was right. *I was ripped by the best!*"

We both laughed.

DIALING FOR DOLLARS

"Would you be interested in a pair of imperforate ten-cent crossed-flag stamps?" the voice on the phone asked. The call came in on my toll-free number just at closing.

"Perhaps," I answered. "Coil or sheet stamps?" The coil variety was quite common. The sheet stamp, much more scarce.

"Sheet."

"Imperf on all sides?" The sheet stamp error existed in two forms: horizontal pairs imperforate between and completely imperforate pairs. The completely imperf variety was the scarcer of the two.

"Yes, imperf all around."

"Vertical pair?" Completely imperforate sheet stamps are collected in vertical pairs in order to distinguish them from imperf coil pairs. The vertical pair, imperforate on all sides, was a valuable error.

"It can be," the caller said, "if that's the way you want it."

"What do you mean by that?" I asked.

"I've got the whole sheet. I could cut it any way you want, or better yet, sell you the whole thing. What will you give me for it?"

Now, he had my attention. An entire sheet offered considerably more possibilities than a single pair. Nevertheless, I was reluctant to make an offer. Errors are tricky. Their value depends entirely on how many others of the same issue surface. Sometimes, the same error surfaces in several places across the country at about the same time. At that moment, I had no idea how many others might exist.

"How much do you want for it?" I asked.

"How about a thousand bucks?" he answered unhesitatingly. The price seemed reasonable. The sheet would yield 50 pairs, which worked out to $20 a pair. The mystery man appeared ready to do business, a fact that surprised me because error deals are usually more difficult to close.

"You're asking a thousand dollars for the whole sheet?" I reiterated, to verify that his quote was for the entire sheet and not just a single pair.

"Yup."

"Well, that's not an unreasonable price," I said, wondering what he knew that I didn't. I'm always suspicious of a deal that goes too smoothly.

Then he said, "What would you pay for a whole pad?"

A whole pad! I almost dropped the phone. Lucky is the person who finds even one imperf sheet in a lifetime. How could someone be so fortunate as to find a complete pad of 100 sheets?

"You mean you went to the post office, bought a sealed pad of ten-cent stamps, then opened it and discovered they were all imperforate?" By its sheer magnitude, one hundred imperforate sheets was the most astounding error discovery I had ever heard of. It was beyond imagining. How many individuals buy unopened pads to begin with? Very few. And of those, what are the odds that all 100 sheets would be imperforate? Infinitesimally small. Astonished as I was, his next comment astounded me even more.

"No, I didn't buy the pad," he said. I could almost hear him chuckle at my astonishment. "I'm supposed to burn them. Ten pads of imperforate crossed-flags came in for destruction. I burned nine of them, but I decided to keep one for myself. A little bonus, you might say. Besides, I thought it would please you collectors. I know how much you dig errors. Listen, I'll make you a real sweet deal—five grand for the whole pad."

I couldn't believe my ears.

"Anything else you might be interested in?" he asked. "I get lots of weird stuff in here—imperfs, messed up colors, you name it. Last week, I got a batch of imperf crossed-flags with the blue missing. Could you use something like that?"

It sounded like an error dealer's dream contact. He could supply almost anything—in quantity. Unfortunately, what he was doing was completely illegal. My mind raced. Possibilities stampeded in all directions. I didn't know what to say.

"You still there?" he asked after a moment.

"Yes." I stammered. "Sorry. It's just that you don't get a call like this every day."

"No problem," he chuckled. "Real mind-boggling, isn't it? Kinda like winning the lottery."

"You *could* say that."

"So, are you interested in the imperf pad for five grand?" he pressed.

"I suppose," I replied, mentally trying to get my feet on the ground. "Why don't you send it to me, and if it's as you say, I'll send you a check right away by return mail."

"Get real," he scoffed. "When I see the green, you get the stamps. I'll fly to Denver, meet you at the airport. Bring five thousand in cash—I'm talking greenbacks, no checks—and the pad is yours. I'll get right back on the plane and be back in Asheville the same night."

"That's a lot of cash to carry around," I hedged, then added, "It's getting late. Give me your phone number. Let me think it over. I'll get back to you in the morning."

He chuckled his response as if amused by my apparent dull-wittedness. "Look, what I'm doing is highly illegal. I can't give you my phone number. I can't tell you my name. I can't tell you where I work. All I can do is sell you the pad of imperfs. You bring five grand in cash to the airport, and I give you the stamps. It's that simple. Now, do you want to do business or not?"

Again, my mind raced. The man on the other end of the line was a thief. Once he hung up, there would be no way of contacting him again. I tried desperately to think of something to say to keep him on the line. I decided my best chance was to play along.

"Okay, five thousand is certainly a reasonable figure. When could you fly in? What airline? Where will I meet you? How will I recognize you?" I blurted out the questions with no real strategy. I'd just have to go with the flow.

"Slow down, pal," he said. "I'll have to check with the airlines and call you back tomorrow. Remember, it's got to be cash. I want twenties and fifties."

"Okay, okay. Say, I could probably use some of the other stuff you mentioned," I added lamely, trying to give him more incentive to call back.

"All in good time," he replied. "We'll see how this first deal goes. Listen, I've got to go now. I'll get back to you tomorrow."

"What time tomorrow?"

"As soon as I find out how to get to Denver and back."

"Okay, don't forget."

"I won't." And with that, the line went dead. It's funny how a person always thinks of the things he could have said after the tumult of the moment has passed. I'd been nervous and hesitant. I couldn't shake the feeling that I'd played it badly. Had my nervousness spooked him? I hoped not.

I fumbled through the business cards in my desk drawer until I found the card of the Secret Service agent who had walked into my office several weeks earlier.

He'd been dressed in a conservative blue suit and looked for all the world like a successful businessman.

"How can I help you?" I'd asked, hoping he would ask to see some high-value Columbians or Zeppelins.

Instead, he flashed his credentials and announced, "Secret Service. Can I have a word with you?"

"Sure."

"Have you seen these stamps?" He showed me a photocopy of an uncut sheet of 13-cent Liberty Bell booklet panes. The individual booklet panes were perforated, but the sheet was imperforate between panes. In normal production, cuts would have been made between panes to separate them into individual booklet panes. Looking at the photocopy, it was easy to see that, if this sheet were separated into individual booklet panes along the perforations, the resulting panes would appear imperforate between.

"Yes," I replied. I had been offered the sheet a few weeks before, but declined. "Why are you looking for it?"

"It was stolen from the Bureau of Engraving and Printing. We're trying to locate it. Where did you see it?"

I gave him the name of the dealer who had shown it to me. He thanked me and left.

Now, card in hand, I called the agent. "We met a few weeks back," I reminded him. "A man just offered me a large quantity of stolen stamps. I played along with him. He wouldn't give me his name, but he's supposed to call back tomorrow to close the deal." I filled him in on the details and how the caller had admitted he was stealing error stamps.

"Remember that sheet of stamps I showed you?" the agent asked.

"Sure."

"We think it came out of Asheville, also. Your caller might be the same guy. We contacted the dealer who offered you the Liberty Bell sheet. He'd purchased it from another dealer. The other dealer purchased it from a man who showed up with it at a stamp show, but didn't give a name. It's quite possible that we're dealing with one individual here. We think he's responsible for stealing and selling several items recently."

"Are the dealers who bought the stamps in trouble?"

"No. They cooperated fully, and we're satisfied that they had no prior knowledge that the sheet was stolen. They're not being charged. However, it's a crime to receive stolen stamps if you're aware they're stolen.

"About this fellow who called you," he continued. "When he calls back, agree to meet him whenever he wants, agree to pay whatever he wants. Just set up a meeting. Then, give me a call—day or night—and we'll arrange a welcoming committee. That's all there is to it."

I couldn't get to sleep that night. Thoughts of the coming sting buzzed around and around like Indy 500 racecars. I rehearsed what I'd say. "I'll meet you at the gate. Yes, I've got the cash—twenties and fifties, just like you said. What else have you got? Can we come to an arrangement, you know, for a steady supply?" I wanted the thief to think he'd found the ideal customer.

Waiting for sleep to come, I visualized how the sting might unfold.

I see his plane taxiing up to the gate. It's late at night, but the terminal is bright inside and bathed in pale yellow floodlight outside. Parallel blue runway lights, looking eerie and other-worldly, run from the brightly lit terminal apron and converge in cool, velvety darkness more than a mile distant. I stand at the window-wall, watching the ramp-lead use orange-tipped flashlights to motion the aircraft to a halt. Jet engines whine down, and, in the light of the cockpit, I see the pilot pull off his headphones. Inside the plane, a flight attendant pops open the forward door and waits for the motorized gate to roll over and kiss the fuselage.

I move away from the plate glass window and out into the main concourse aisle directly in front of gate B9. I don't want to miss the imperf man. I glance behind me. All is in order. Two Secret Service agents wait across the aisle, pretending to be engrossed in conversation. Another, seated in the waiting area, reads a newspaper. The last, wearing an airline windbreaker and carrying a clipboard, lingers near the arrival gate door. If necessary, he'll block the suspect if he tries to run back onto the plane.

The door at the gate opens, and weary travelers begin to stream off the plane. Grandparents bend down to hug waiting grandchildren. Husbands and wives stop momentarily to embrace, then hurry off in a hubbub of conversation to claim their baggage. Lovers rush to meet, arms outstretched, then lose themselves for a long, delirious moment in the passion of reuniting. And tired businessmen—ties loose, jackets on one arm, carry-on luggage slung over their shoulders— don't stop at all.

The plane empties, and I wait, scanning the passengers for any sign of the imperf man. *What if he decided not to come?* I can't worry about it. After what seems like a hundred people, the stream slows to a trickle. The plane is almost empty. At last, the imperf walks out. He's wearing Levis, a checked shirt, and a navy blue windbreaker. He carries no luggage, just an overstuffed brown envelope.

I'm holding a stamp catalogue, our prearranged recognition signal. Smiling, he walks up and says, "You must be Steve."

"That's right. I'm afraid I didn't get your name."

He chuckles. "I didn't give it. Can't afford to. You bring the money?"

"Yes." I pat my jacket pocket. "You bring the stamps?"

"Got 'em right here. Let's do business." He leads the way to a deserted waiting area across the aisle from gate B9. The lights are turned low. In the dim semi-darkness, he pulls the corner of the manila envelope back. Red, white, and blue imperf crossed-flag stamps peek out.

"I want to check the whole pad," I say.

"Sure, no problem." He hands it to me. I pull the stamps out. The pad is solid and weighty. I flip though it. Not a perf to be seen.

"Looks good," I say, then reach into my jacket for the fat envelope of cash. That's the signal. The agents start to move. As soon as the money touches his hand, they'll grab him.

"Here you go," I say, handing over the envelope. The imperf man smiles with expectation, but before he can open it, the two nearest Secret Service agents reach us.

"Stretch your arms out from your sides and don't move," one of them commands. A dark wrinkle crosses the imperf man's brow, as comprehension begins to dawn.

"Secret Service," the agent says. "You're under arrest. Move slowly to the wall and place your hands on it."

They pat him down, cuff him, and lead him away. The agent in charge turns to me and says, "Thanks, Mr. Datz. You've performed a fine service for your country. You can be proud of that." I bask in the warm sunlight of his compliment.

The scene replayed itself several times. Later, long after midnight, I finally lapsed into sleep.

The following day, I waited and waited, unable to concentrate on the simplest task. Each time the phone rang, I jumped at it. But each time, it was just another routine call. By five o'clock, I was a nervous wreck, totally exhausted. A lack of sleep combined with mounting tension from waiting all day for the big call had taken its toll.

Then, just at five o'clock, the phone rang. The light on the 800 line blinked. It had to be the imperf man. He'd called at the same time the day before. Why hadn't I known that he'd wait until the same time to call today? I'd worried all day for nothing.

"May I help you?" I asked, waiting to hear the imperf man's voice.

"Hi. I'm Carla with Fly-Right Travel. You've just won a travel shopping spree worth one thousand dollars. Aren't you excited!?"

I leaned back in my chair . . . stretched out for a long moment . . . exhaled deeply. The day's tension suddenly drained out of me. I felt like a deflated balloon. I didn't know whether to laugh or be angry.

"Thanks, Carla," I said, "but I'll have to pass on your Fly-By-Night Travel spree."

"Not Fly-By-Night," she said earnestly, correcting me. *"Fly-Right."*

"Thanks anyway, Carla. It's been a long day. The only trip I'm taking is home and to sleep." I plopped the phone down, turned out the lights, and headed home.

I knew I wasn't going to hear from the imperf man.

The imperf man never called back. Not the next day, not ever. I was disappointed. I'd looked forward to participating in the sting. What had spooked him? Instinct? Caution? I never found out.

Sometime later, I learned from the Secret Service that they had arrested an employee at the destruction facility in Asheville. The arrest resulted from other leads. It seems that the suspect had sold printer's waste to a variety of dealers. The Secret Service pursued the leads, tracked them back to their source, set up surveillance, and eventually arrested the culprit. He turned out to be the same man who had sold the imperf Liberty Bell booklet panes.

The Secret Service thought it highly likely that he was the same individual who had called me with the imperf ten-cent crossed-flag sheets.

The imperf man, as I call him, was tried, convicted, and sentenced to two years in prison.

THE STUFF OF DREAMS

"My name is Donald K. Garrity," said the man who walked into my office, extending his right hand. "I have some very unusual stamps. They should literally be worth a fortune to the right buyer."

"Have a seat. Let's see what you've got," I said, anxious to see his stamps, but doubting his remark was little more than a figurative exaggeration.

Garrity appeared to be in his early fifties, of medium build and height. His tanned features reminded me of that leathery look peculiar to ranchers who have spent too many years in the sun and weather. He wore his hair short. Its brown had just begun to yield to gray. He seated himself, unbuttoning a sand-colored sports coat that looked new, but slightly out of style, as if purchased years before but not often worn.

From a dilapidated piece of luggage that was too large to be an attaché case, but too small to be a suitcase, he extracted a box of glassines and placed it on my desk. It seemed like he took special care to close the case after removing the box, as if it might contain something he didn't want me to see.

I let my thumb riffle across the top of the snugly packed glassines, occasionally pulling one out. Glassine after glassine contained imperfs, part perfs, inverted overprints and surcharges, double and triple overprints and surcharges, hundreds of exotic—perhaps even rare—Chinese stamps. It was not the kind of material found in standard catalogues. The box looked like a specialist's gold mine. My skepticism began to melt.

During my preliminary inspection, Donald Garrity sat back in his chair and watched me impassively.

"Very unusual, to say the least," I said at last, looking up, still struggling to comprehend the significance of the contents of the box. I possessed no specialized knowledge of Chinese stamps, but the abundance of esoteric material made me suspect that the collection might, indeed, be valuable, or, at least, highly salable. I was interested but not awed. Enough instinctive skepticism lingered to prevent that.

Garrity acknowledged my remark with a nod. He pushed himself slightly more upright in his chair, as if I had passed the first test and the meeting could now proceed, the implication being that he didn't want to waste time with someone who couldn't recognize the significance of his stamps.

Stamps can be tricky. No matter how many years you've been in the business, you still come across material whose rarity or value is not immediately apparent. Garrity's stamps could have been worth very little or worth a fortune. I simply didn't know.

I should also point out that after you've been in the stamp business long enough, you develop an instinct for that which holds promise. And if ever a box of stamps exuded the rich, seductive scent of promise, this one did.

"I'm not an expert on Chinese stamps," I said, "but it looks like you've got some pretty good material here."

"I can assure you that they *are* quite rare—and valuable," Garrity said emphatically. He leaned forward, elbows on the arms of his chair. His eyes met mine. "You won't find another collection like it anywhere."

"Probably not," I said. "But how do I know—or you know, for that matter—they're genuine?"

"Oh, they're genuine all right," Garrity said. He leaned further forward and fixed his gaze even more intently. He studied me, as if deciding whether to take me into his confidence or simply gather up the stamps and walk out. The moment stretched, seemed interminably long. Then, he removed a cigarette from the pack of Camels in his shirt pocket and lit it. He spoke as he exhaled, "Well, do you want to do business?"

I was in no position to make an intelligent decision. Still, I didn't want to let a deal slip between my fingers.

"Sure," I said, "but I need to know more about these stamps. Where'd you get them, anyway?"

Garrity leaned back in his chair and slowly rubbed one hand over the top of the other, as if massaging an aching muscle.

"I was very lucky to get them," he allowed. "It's a long story, but one I suppose you should hear. It will help you appreciate their value."

And with that, he began the tale.

"After the Second World War, Chinese currency suffered tremendous inflation that resulted in lots of overprints on stamps. Eventually, the currency was revalued, which, again, resulted in lots of overprints. Civil war raged across the countryside. Provincial overprints and surcharges abounded.

"A certain Chinese businessman with a keen interest in stamps knew a man who knew a printer. Money changed hands. Stamps that otherwise might have been discarded as printer's waste suddenly found a home. By 1949, Mao's armies had Chiang Kai-shek on the run. The Chinese businessman saw the handwriting on the wall. It was time to leave. His stamps were among the few things he could easily carry out of the country. He fled to Hong Kong, and there sold the stamps to raise cash.

"From the Crown Colony, the stamps made their way to London—exactly how, I don't know. Nor do I know how long they remained in London. I do know that from London the stamps eventually reached Beirut, acquired by an astute stamp dealer who felt he had the ideal client for them—King Farouk of Egypt. Here the story gets a bit murky. At about that time—I think it was 1955—Farouk was deposed and forced to flee the country. In any case, the stamps came into the possession of an Egyptian stamp dealer, who plied his trade from a shop on one of those nameless, narrow streets in Cairo."

Garrity paused to light another cigarette. He leaned back and exhaled slowly, the smoke rising serenely, like a thin white veil. The pause had its dramatic effect. In that moment, a thought flickered across my mind like a scene from an old movie. Garrity's story reminded me of the scene in *The Maltese Falcon* in which Sidney Greenstreet's Casper Gutman explains the origin of the falcon to Humphrey Bogart's Sam Spade. However, Garrity more closely resembled the Joel Cairo character—Peter Lorre—than the portly

Sidney Greenstreet. Garrity, like Lorre, spoke softly and had that same vague air of mystery about him.

The odyssey of the Chinese stamps stirred my imagination. I visualized a man in a trench coat and a wide-brimmed fedora spiriting the stamps from London to Beirut via Istanbul on the Orient Express. I visualized him delivering the stamps to an obese man wearing a maroon fez, a man known only by the enigmatic name "the Egyptian." They sat in high fanback chairs at a small table in a dim, smoke-filled cafe. They smiled cordially at one another and traded polite insincerities. Cash and stamps changed hands. And when the deal was done, they shook hands and departed, vanishing into the night, down narrow, fog-shrouded streets.

I glanced at Garrity through the veil of smoke, but I saw, instead, Joel Cairo—cigarette in hand, relaxed, shrewd, and infinitely inscrutable—looking back at me.

"What happened to the stamps after the Egyptian got them?" I asked. "How did you get them?"

Garrity took another long drag on his cigarette and smiled thinly, almost slyly. "Luck—sheer luck. I was working in Saudi Arabia— petroleum exploration.

"I often made trips to Beirut, Cairo, and Istanbul. I liked seeing the sights, shopping, ferreting out the unusual. I got wind of the Chinese stamps in Beirut—that was back in the sixties, before all the trouble began. Beirut was a beautiful city then, sophisticated, worldly, a city where European and Arabian culture met and mingled." Garrity exhaled another lungful of cigarette smoke, and I sensed from his tone of voice that he missed those days in the Middle East.

"I got wind of the stamps from an old Lebanese stamp dealer by the name of Rashid. We passed a long, pleasant afternoon together one day. We traded stories, laughed, and drank a lot of thick, syrupy Turkish coffee. Rashid was determined to impress me with his importance and his contacts. And the greatest, most enormously important deal of his life was the Chinese stamp deal. The story strutted from his lips, despite his pretense of humility, like a peacock preening its feathers.

"According to Rashid, it was he who was entrusted to deliver the stamps to the Egyptian dealer, who was then supposed to deliver them to Farouk. For this service, Rashid was to receive one of the better stamps of his choice.

"Rashid raved about the collection," Garrity said. "It was magnificent, truly worthy of a king, and he, Rashid, had the great honor of being entrusted to deliver it to Cairo, which he did. In the middle of his story, Rashid took a blue leather stock book from his desk drawer and showed me the stamp he had been given for his services. At the time, I didn't know much about Chinese stamps, but I wish I had tried to buy it from him. If I'm not mistaken, it's a genuine rarity. It's no doubt lost today, what with the civil war and all. And who knows, Rashid is probably dead by now."

My eyes returned to the puzzling box of stamps. I wondered how many rarities it contained. I wondered how, of all the stamp dealers in the world, fate had brought it to me.

"Had it not been for the stamp in the blue leather stock book," Garrity continued, "I would have shrugged off Rashid's tale as just an egotistical exaggeration. But Rashid's stamp got me thinking that the rest of the Chinese stamps might still be in Cairo.

"Rashid told me the Egyptian's name was Hassan Hagazi," Garrity said. "I asked if Hagazi was still in business. Rashid answered with a shrug: he might be or he might not be. Rashid couldn't be sure. He had been out of contact for many years.

"I thought it a little odd," Garrity said. "There are so few stamp dealers in the Middle East, one would think they'd remain in contact. I thought, perhaps Rashid didn't want me to make contact with Hagazi for some reason. Or perhaps he had made up the whole story.

"I asked Rashid if Hagazi had delivered the stamps to Farouk. He wasn't sure. He shrugged and commented that with Farouk dead, who knew where the stamps were now.

"The thing about a mystery, it can become irresistible," Garrity continued. "I had to follow it up. The next time I was in Cairo, I went looking for Hagazi, and found him. It was easier than I'd anticipated. He was still in business. His shop was small and dimly lit, and he was much older than I'd expected.

"I mentioned Rashid's name. Asked Hagazi if he remembered the man. Explained that I was interested in Chinese stamps and curious about the story Rashid had told me.

"Yes, he remembered Rashid. Yes, he had delivered the stamps to Farouk. It had been a privilege to do a favor for the king. 'Farouk was a wonderful man . . . a generous man!' Hagazi proclaimed, in a voice at once reverent and nostalgic."

Garrity paused long enough to light another Camel. The afternoon wore on, but I didn't notice the time pass. Garrity's tale was smooth and spellbinding.

"When Farouk was suddenly forced to flee the country," Garrity said, "Hagazi, again, found himself in possession of the Chinese stamps. Farouk instructed him to hold them for safekeeping until things settled down, but Hagazi worried about being caught with them. He worried for no particular reason, other than the climate of fear that followed Nassar's revolution. He decided it was best to get them out of the country. They ended up in Saudi Arabia with a trusted friend who owed Farouk a favor. As fate would have it, the stamps remained in the possession of the Saudi—whose name I'm not at liberty to reveal—until I came along."

Garrity reached forward and, hefting the box of glassines to emphasize his point, said, "You know, it's a miracle that these stamps are here in front of us right now." He pulled his lips tight against his teeth, raised his eyebrows, and sucked in a great breath of air. He exhaled a sigh, nodding his head slowly in a rocking motion, as if lost in the sheer wondrousness of the thought.

I found myself nodding along in unconscious agreement. *Yes*, I thought, *it's a miracle*. I was totally engrossed in the tale, which seemed to please Garrity.

He smiled and gently returned the box to the desktop.

"Hagazi said that time had passed, that, no doubt, the Saudi felt the stamps belonged to him now, if only by virtue of the favor owed. Hagazi said that his own responsibility to Farouk had ended when the king died. The Saudi had the stamps, but Hagazi wouldn't tell me his name. He felt honor-bound to respect the man's privacy.

"I left Cairo disappointed," Garrity said. "I'd run up against a stone wall. I figured that was the end of it.

"I returned to Riyadh. Forgot all about the stamps. In the course of my work, I've met a lot of people, eaten many a meal cross-legged in an Arab tent, and spent many a night under the stars out in the desert, a million miles from nowhere. I don't remember why, but one evening the subject of stamps came up. My host remarked that his brother owned some stamps that once had belonged to King Farouk.

"I felt like I'd been kicked by a camel," Garrity said. "I dared not hope that these were the very same stamps I'd so lucklessly chased. Would the brother object to my seeing the stamps, I wanted to know.

My friend agreed to ask—if it meant that much to me. I assured him it did. He laughed. 'You westerners,' he said. 'What strange people you are. What's so important about a few little bits of paper? But if it pleases you, I will ask.'

"Time went by," Garrity said. "Perhaps my host forgot to ask his brother about the stamps. I don't know. I didn't press the issue. Eventually, I happened to meet the brother at a big get-together. He looked like someone out of *Lawrence of Arabia*, wearing a flowing white desert robe and carrying a beautiful dagger tucked in his waistband, the kind with a rhinoceros-horn handle. Of course, I asked him about the stamps.

" 'Yes, I remember the stamps,' he said. 'Hagazi—the nervous little Egyptian—left them with me. He said they belonged to Farouk. Hagazi was anxious to find a safe place for them. I agreed to keep them. Farouk had favored my family with a kindness once. It was the least I could do to return the favor. The king was a foolish man, wasting so much time on hobbies and women. No wonder he lost his throne. But that was his business. Mine is in the desert. I never heard from Farouk about the stamps. He's dead now, so I guess they're mine. They don't look like much to me . . . but then, what do I know of stamps? If you're interested, you can have them. You've been a good friend to my brother. He has always spoken highly of you. I make a gift of them to you. Enjoy them in good health.'

"I couldn't believe my good fortune," Garrity said. "The stamps dropped into my lap, and I've had them ever since."

Garrity stubbed out his cigarette in an ashtray already brimming with butts, the residue of his afternoon's story. He had exhaled his long, convoluted story one puff at a time. Cigarette smoke hung in layers like thin cirrus clouds that, with the growing dimness of the late afternoon, gave the room a dark, atmospheric effect. We sat silently for a long moment, Garrity and I, like actors in a vintage film noir, each waiting for the other to break the silence. The mood created by Garrity's incredible tale had, in my imagination, transformed the office into a setting of murky ambiance, like an ageless coffeehouse in Cairo, Beirut, or Istanbul. And in the failing light, Garrity's sand-colored blazer was close enough to white to resemble a tropical suit. The effect was complete.

Garrity, the master storyteller, sat impassively, watching and waiting for the craftsmanship of his tale to work its magic on me. And it did. I wanted the stamps—badly.

"How much do you want for the lot?" I asked.

"I'm not sure," Garrity replied. "I was hoping you could give me some idea of its value."

I suspected the box might be worth a lot of money, but exactly how much, I didn't know. I also sensed that Garrity had a figure in mind, but wouldn't reveal it.

"I don't have the expertise to judge either the genuineness or the value of your stamps," I said. Garrity raised his eyebrows ever so slightly, but said nothing. "To be fair to both of us, I need to know more about them. Would you object to someone else looking at them?"

"No," he replied casually, shaking his head, reaching for another cigarette. "Who'd you have in mind?"

"I think I know just the man. He lives in the Upper Midwest—"

"I'm not going to leave the stamps or ship them," Garrity interrupted. "He'll have to come here. Nothing personal, you understand. Just too many years in the desert."

I nodded. "Let me call him tomorrow and see if he'll fly out. I'll get back to you just as soon as I have an answer. Of course, I don't want to put him to the trouble of making the trip if you're not ready to sell. There can be no misunderstanding on this point." I looked Garrity straight in the eye. "You are ready to close a deal, provided we can agree on a price?"

Garrity didn't so much as blink. "Of course . . . provided we can agree on a price," he said, pushing himself up in the chair and smiling a thin, half-smile, then adding, "Reasonable men can always find common ground . . . can they not?"

And that's the last thing I remember about the meeting. Donald Garrity left, or, perhaps, simply faded into the lingering smoke and gathering dusk. I was much too preoccupied with how to put a deal together to notice.

I didn't sleep much that night. The stamps kept me awake. Garrity's story played itself again and again in the insomniac theater of my mind. What a potentially fantastic collection! How much was it worth? . . . $50,000? . . . $100,000? . . . $500,000? How much profit could be made? How best to sell it? Break it up or offer it intact? A thousand eager, boisterous possibilities competed for attention. They persisted well into the early morning hours, until slept finally came.

I had heard that the man I had in mind to expertize Garrity's stamps—I'll call him David O. Mayfield—was quite knowledgeable. I knew little about him; however, others in the trade whose opinions I valued spoke highly of him. So I called him, described the stamps, and gave him a brief synopsis of their origin. He hadn't heard of the collection and was completely unaware of its existence.

"Sounds like a wonderful lot," he said on the phone. "I'd love to see it."

"That's just what I had in mind," I said. "I need someone knowledgeable to look the stamps over, confirm that they're genuine, and give me some idea of their value. Of course, I'll pay you for your trouble, or if you have clients for the stamps, I'd be more than happy to discuss some arrangement that would benefit us both."

"Set up a meeting," Mayfield said. "If the stamps are as good as they sound, I've got advanced collectors who'll pay handsomely for them."

"Well, the collection looks like it ought to be worth big bucks," I said, "but then again, I really don't know what I'm looking at."

"Don't worry," Mayfield assured me. "I know that material inside out."

So I didn't worry. I arranged for the three of us to meet the following week.

Donald Garrity arrived promptly, wearing his sand-colored blazer, carrying his attaché-case-that-was-not-really-an-attaché-case in one hand and a Camel cigarette in the other. We made ourselves comfortable around my large desk. Garrity eased the box of glassines out of his attaché case and placed it on the desk in front of Mayfield.

Mayfield went right to work. Using long stamp tongs, he carefully extracted one stamp after another. He squinted, totally absorbed in his task, scrutinizing random samples under a ten-power loupe, muttering impressions *sotto voce*, "Interesting . . . hmm, didn't know that existed imperf . . . a double overprint by itself is very rare, let alone multiples . . ." At one point he looked up at Garrity and said, "This *is* truly excellent material."

"I can see you're a man with an eye for rare stamps," Garrity replied, "a connoisseur who appreciates quality." Mayfield reacted to the flattery like a cat being stroked. He leaned into the compliment and all but purred. Garrity smiled his vague, knowing-yet-unrevealing, poker-player's smile and took another drag on his Camel.

Mayfield worked more quickly as he progressed through the box, taking less and less time with each stamp. It was as if he'd reached a verdict and was just checking to see how many stamps the box contained.

"I'm really quite awed," Mayfield said as he finished up. "I've never seen so much Chinese specialty material in one place before. Looks like it came right from the printer."

Garrity chuckled. "Supposedly, it did," he said. Then without any prompting, he launched into the saga of the stamps. He paused now and then to light a Camel, take a drag, then exhale slowly. Mayfield listened intently, captivated by the mystique of the convoluted tale. And why shouldn't he be? Stamp dealers rarely hear so colorful an adventure, rarely come across so promising a deal. At the same time, Garrity enjoyed telling the story and enjoyed its effect on Mayfield.

It was nearly lunchtime when he finished. For Mayfield, the tale was the icing on the cake. He was beside himself with excitement. I asked Garrity to excuse us for a few minutes so we could discuss the stamps. Garrity smiled knowingly and said, "Sure." Then he headed for the reception area, lighting another Camel as he went.

"I've never seen anything like it!" Mayfield gushed. "It's truly rare! You virtually never see it, yet he's got it in multiples and combinations! It's absolutely fabulous!"

"Are they genuine?" I asked.

"There might be a few problem items, but, overall, the lot looks good to me."

"What should I offer?"

"Well, it's difficult to know exactly," Mayfield said, "but I don't think you could go wrong at ten thousand dollars. Do you think he'd take ten thousand?"

"I don't know. We'll just have to ask. Ten thousand doesn't sound like much if the stamps are as good as you say . . ."

"Well, that's the trouble with this kind of material," Mayfield said. "There's no catalogue value to go by, no way of really knowing what it's worth other than to take a chance. The lot looks pretty good, but by the same token, it pays to be a little cautious in case it contains a few clunkers."

"You mean fakes might be a problem?"

"No, not really. There might be a few bad stamps in the group, but nothing to be concerned about."

"What's the very most you'd pay?"

"No more than twelve thousand five hundred dollars."

"You yourself would be willing to pay twelve thousand five hundred for the lot?" I asked, to make sure I'd heard him correctly.

"Yes, it's worth at least that much. Listen, I have some great potential customers for this stuff. I'd be happy to take the lot right now—if we make a deal—and pay you a commission, of course."

"Thanks," I said, "but if the lot is as good as you think it is, I want to participate in the profits." I had no desire forego significantly larger profits for the sake of a small, albeit quick, commission.

Mayfield's unbridled enthusiasm led me to believe they were probably worth more than he let on.

"Okay," he said, I have no problem working with you on the lot." He'd begun rubbing his hands together unconsciously. "I've got buyers who'll fight tooth and nail over it." Mayfield was as excited as a child on Christmas morning.

I considered. I didn't have a ready market for Garrity's stamps; Mayfield did.

"Can you move the whole collection as a unit?" I asked. I wanted to keep things simple. Breaking the collection up and selling individual items would entail a lot of record keeping and only complicate the arrangement.

"I think so," Mayfield said.

"How fast could you turn it?"

"A week, if I'm lucky, couple of weeks or a month, if I'm not. It's good stuff. It'll go away quickly."

"How much could you get for it?"

"I don't know, but I'd probably start at twenty-five thousand . . . maybe more. I'll have to check it out more thoroughly before I can give you a definite figure. Who knows, if I found the right buyer—someone with oil money for instance—I might be able to get a hundred thousand. Stranger things have happened. On the downside, it ought to be worth at least fifteen to twenty thousand dollars."

"All right," I said, "I'll buy the stamps, and we'll split profits fifty-fifty on anything you sell. Fair enough?" And before he could answer, I added, "But your people will have to act fast. I don't want to tie up my money indefinitely."

"No problem. You've got yourself a deal."

"Now, let's see if we can buy ourselves some stamps," I said, opening the office door to invite Garrity back in.

"Gentlemen," Garrity said, "have you made a decision?" He strolled casually back into the office. He seemed perfectly relaxed.

I had a feeling that we were in the calm water just ahead of swift rapids and that negotiating with Garrity would be like shooting whitewater in a kayak.

"We're interested," I said. "How much do you want for the lot?"

"Make me an offer," he replied, sounding almost disinterested. However, I took it for shrewdness. He had, no doubt, honed his negotiating skills in many a hard-fought deals with crafty, hard-bargaining Middle East merchants. I admired his coolness.

"Seventy-five hundred dollars," I said, watching his face to measure his reaction.

"You've got to be kidding!" he snorted.

"No, I'm serious. The material is nice, but esoteric. You yourself know it's not listed in catalogues. Its value is uncertain, a big question mark. I've lost a fair amount of money on eye-popping material that proved to be considerably worth less than it first appeared."

"Oh, come on," Garrity's tone was incredulous, "These stamps have the potential to be worth big money, maybe even six figures."

"I wouldn't go that far—"

"Look, I'm not going to let it go for a pittance," Garrity said emphatically.

"How about ten thousand dollars?" I asked. "I'm afraid I can't be as wildly optimistic about the value of your stamps as you are, especially when my money's at stake."

"How much do think they're worth retail?" he asked.

"I'm not sure. Besides, I make it a policy never to discuss anticipated retail prices with sellers. Nor do I trouble them with my problems—the cost of my overhead, the years of work to build up a clientele, or the risk of loss. The market is full of pitfalls and hazards."

"I'm sure it is," Garrity said. "On the other hand, a collection like this comes along once in a man's lifetime—if he's lucky. I'll never get another like it, so I want to get the most I can for it." He paused and lit another Camel, then said, "There *are* other dealers. You're the first I've contacted."

"And they might well offer less," I said.

"Or more," he countered.

"It's possible," I admitted.

"On the other hand, David is one of the leading dealers in the country for this kind of material. I have to respect his opinion about its value. That's what I'm basing my offer on. We're anxious to do business. If we thought your stamps justified more money, we'd offer more. As far as the collection yielding six figures, that possibility is remote at best—a real long shot."

"There are always plenty of buyers at the camel market," Garrity said coolly, unemotionally. "Perhaps it's time to let them have a look at the goods."

I'd hoped that we could do business for cash, with no strings attached, but I sensed it was not to be. Garrity was about to take a walk, and I didn't want to lose the deal.

"Well, we have an interesting problem here," I said. "We—all of us—believe the stamps are valuable, but we don't know precisely how valuable. Ten thousand dollars? . . . twenty thousand? . . . a hundred thousand? We're not sure. You don't want to sell too cheaply; we don't want to pay too much. How to solve the problem?" I paused, waited for a reaction from Garrity, but his face remained inscrutable.

"I'll give you ten thousand for the collection, and one-third of any profits over twenty-five thousand. You'll have some cash up front, regardless of what the collection ultimately sells for. And if it turns out to be worth big bucks, you'll share in the profits."

"The idea has merit," Garrity said, looking more interested. "But one-third hardly seems fair. If anyone should get one-third, you should, not me. After all, I found the stamps."

"True, but we have the customers . . . and they didn't come free. It costs money to run a business. Your share is clear profit, ours is subject to expenses."

Garrity leaned forward in his chair. He stubbed out his cigarette, carefully, thoughtfully.

"Fifteen thousand up front," he said, "and fifty-fifty on everything over twenty-five thousand."

"Twelve thousand, five hundred, period," I said. "No profit sharing. *Or* ten thousand cash, plus fifty percent of everything over twenty-five thousand."

Garrity paused. At that point I smelled a deal in the air. Garrity was simply bargaining for the best terms he could get.

"Make it twelve-five and fifty percent, and you've got yourself a deal."

"I really don't want to do that," I replied. "I'll tell you why. Most guys wouldn't lay out a dime on a profit-sharing deal. They'd want you to consign the stamps, then they'd pay you as they go. On the other hand, you'll walk out of here with ten thousand bucks in your pocket. You're guaranteed that much—win, lose or draw. We've already agreed on the fifty-fifty split, so there's no argument there.

"Another thing, we've got the best customers for the material, the collectors who'll pay top dollar. The more the material brings, the more there is to split—right? Maximizing profit is the name of the game.

"Finally, if the collection is as good as you think it is, the real money's to be made in the profit above twenty-five thousand dollars. So, why are we quibbling over a couple thousand dollars? The offer I've made you is more than fair."

Garrity narrowed his gaze and moved his hand to his chin. His face remained expressionless, as unyielding as the desert. I wasn't sure he'd heard a word I'd said, or if he had, that he was persuaded. Mayfield fidgeted; negotiating made him uncomfortable. Had it been up to him, I was sure he would have paid twelve-five and settled for one-third of the profits. We waited.

When Garrity finally spoke, his words were anticlimactic and without emotion: "Okay, ten thousand cash up front, plus fifty percent of everything over twenty-five thousand."

"All right," I said, "we've got a deal." I stood and reached across the desk to shake his hand. Mayfield, too, was on his feet. He pumped Garrity's hand so hard you'd have thought Garrity had just saved his life.

I drew up an agreement outlining the terms we had agreed to and attached it to my standard philatelic bill of sale. Garrity signed the documents, and I presented him with a check for ten thousand dollars.

"A pleasure gentlemen—a real pleasure." And with that Donald K. Garrity departed.

An elated Mayfield flew home with the stamps.

It was a busy time for me. I didn't think much about him or the stamps. I trusted that he was busy finding the right buyer and making us a tidy profit.

After a ten days had passed without word, I gave him a call.

"How are things going?" I asked, expecting to hear good news.

"Not as well as we'd hoped, I'm afraid." His voice lacked the buoyancy it had had on the day we closed the deal.

"Oh? What's the problem?"

"The first fellow I showed the collection to passed on it. He said it contained too many problem stamps."

"Problem stamps?"

"He felt that some of the key pieces were dubious."

"He was probably trying to hammer you on the price," I said.

"I don't think so. He's a specialist. I'm sure he knows what he's talking about. Besides, price wasn't the object. He just didn't want the lot. He sounded real gun-shy."

I wasn't convinced. Sometimes, buyers say funny things. Maybe he just couldn't afford the collection, but rather than admit it, he cast aspersions on the lot to save face.

"How many items was he unsure about?" I asked.

"He didn't go into detail, just said the lot contained too many potential problem items."

That was bad news, indeed. Still, I couldn't believe the lot was as shaky as Mayfield's customer hinted.

"Where's the lot now?" I asked.

"With another potential buyer. I've been meaning to call him, just didn't want to rush him."

"Why don't you nudge him? If he's not interested, let's move on to the next customer."

"Okay, I'll give him a call."

"Let me know as soon as you've talked to him. The way you talked when you were out here, I thought the lot would be gone by now."

Mayfield sounded uncomfortable on the phone, and rather vague. Something didn't feel right. Nothing I could put my finger on, but I was beginning to have qualms. I was also annoyed by Mayfield's lack of speed in moving the deal forward and by his sudden equivocation. I was annoyed because it was my money on the line—not his. Annoyed because it was his opinion that had set the whole deal in motion. He was the expert.

Mayfield called back with more bad news. The second buyer, too, had passed, expressing the same reservations as buyer number one.

"He felt the lot contained too many problem stamps," Mayfield said. "But he might be interested in the collection at around ten thousand dollars—purely for reference and study."

"You said the stamps looked okay the day you checked them out," I said, trying to restrain my growing irritation.

"Well, they did . . . at first glance. But I was feeling a little under the weather that morning. Maybe it was jet lag . . . or something I ate. I just wasn't as sharp as I normally am . . . I was somewhat distracted . . ." Mayfield offered feebly.

You're supposed to be the expert, I thought. Yet when the chips were down, you didn't seem to know what you were doing. Then, to add insult to injury, you gloss over your incompetence with lame excuses.

"Send the lot back right away," I said tersely, holding my anger in check.

"My customer might be interested in parts of the lot—"

"Send the whole thing back intact, *right away!*"

"Okay, no need to get testy."

"Easy for you to say. Your money's not riding on the deal!"

"Okay, okay," he sighed. It was clear that Mayfield wanted to wash his hands of the whole affair. The situation had become a little too unpleasant for him.

The turn of events disappointed me. As I hung up, my opinion of David O. Mayfield dropped to zero. I wanted nothing further to do with him.

The stamps arrived a few days later. By that time, Garrity's collection had lost its luster. I don't consider myself superstitious, but when a deal begins to feel wrong—a friend calls it bad karma—it's time to wholesale it, salvage what you can, and move on.

According to Mayfield's friends, the lot contained some problem stamps—Mayfield's sanitary euphemisms for fakes—but how many was unclear. The lot contained too many stamps to make it practical to have them individually expertized. In any case, Mayfield's second customer seemed to think the lot was worth at least $10,000—my original outlay—so I decided to try to cash out for that.

Stamp dealer Gary Hertz eventually bought the collection. I explained what had been told to me, that it contained some spurious material, although I didn't know precisely which stamps or how many. Hertz didn't seem too concerned. He felt confident that he could do well with it, and I was glad to be rid of it.

"Remember the Chinese lot you sold me about a month ago?" Hertz asked, hailing me in one of the aisles at COMPEX in Chicago. Before I could answer, he continued, "The stamps are all phony!"

"What!"

"The stamps are phony. At least, every one that's worth any real money."

I was stunned. "How do you know? Who told you?"

"I've had a couple of people look at it," Hertz said. He mentioned the name of one expert, whom I'll call Glen. "I mounted the whole lot in new Lighthouse stock books. Glen went through them stamp by stamp, made a red mark by each fake. Look." He opened the stock book so I could see. "See for yourself," he said, pointing to the red marks. I flipped through stock book. Nearly every stamp was marked in red. Nearly every one, a fake!

A rapid-fire sequence of images, like a montage of film clips, flashed into my consciousness: the ever-so-vaguely smiling Garrity; his intricately woven, masterfully told tale of intrigue, mystery, and fortune; the shadowy Rashid; the mysterious Hagazi; the fortuitous desert rendezvous; the spineless Mayfield; and sadly, my $10,000. And now the party was over. Hertz came back into focus.

"Well," he said, closing the stock book, "what do you think?

Sick at heart, I groped for words, not sure what he meant. Did I agree they were fakes? I had no way of knowing. I had to take his word for it. What was I going to do? I wasn't sure. Had I known the lot consisted mostly of fakes, I would never have bought it, and never have sold it to Hertz.

"I've got five stock books full of fakes," Hertz said. "Steve, the whole lot is a loser. I was kind of hoping you could make an adjustment on it."

"Adjustment?"

"Well, I think it's obvious that the lot isn't worth ten thousand," he said.

Suddenly, the solution became clear to me.

"I'll refund your money," I said. I would stand behind my goods, not worry about how to sidestep the issue as Mayfield had. Hertz wasn't going to stand the loss. Nor was I going to stand the loss. The man responsible—Donald K. Garrity—would.

Hertz didn't stop to question my action. He handed over the remaining stock books, somewhat surprised to be getting a refund.

Back in Denver, on the advice of my attorney, I sent a letter to Garrity setting forth the facts: The stamps are not genuine, and I demand a refund.

Garrity replied through his attorney: The deal is history, and that's all there is to it.

It could be argued that, being a professional, I was in a better position to judge the genuineness of the stamps than the layman, Donald Garrity. After all, I had had my expert—such as he was— examine the stamps. However, Garrity had signed the bill of sale, which contained the clause "the undersigned seller warrants that the property is *genuine in all respects*." And clearly the stamps were not. Garrity had committed himself in writing to stand behind the stamps. And now he would have to do that.

The case headed for court. Garrity's attorney believed they were in a strong position, despite the written warranty in the bill of sale.

My attorney advised me that for evidence I would need to get a written opinion from a reliable expert that the stamps were bogus. So, I sent the stamps away for expertizing.

At that juncture, a crucial development occurred. The expertizer had seen the stamps before. They had been submitted to him months earlier by another stamp dealer. My heart raced when I learned the news. I called the other dealer immediately to confirm what the expertizer had said.

"Yes, I remember the stamps," the dealer said. "They were offered to me about a year ago. Looked like an interesting lot. Too bad they were all fakes."

"Who offered you the lot?" I asked.

"Fellow out west . . . don't remember his name offhand. Why?"

"I bought the stamps, and I'm trying to get my money back. Does the name Garrity ring a bell?"

He thought for a moment. "Yes . . . that sounds right. I told him they were all fakes. He didn't seem too surprised. You bought them, huh?" The dealer sounded vaguely amused.

"Would you be willing to put in writing that Garrity offered you stamps, that you informed him an expert concluded they were fakes?"

"Sure. Why?"

"Because I'm taking Garrity to court."

"No problem."

I was elated that Garrity couldn't plead the injured innocent. He knew the stamps were fake the first day he walked in.

When my attorney heard the news, he said, "That's it! Fraud. A clear-cut case of fraud. Garrity knew the stamps were phony, yet attested to their genuineness on the bill of sale. Open-and-shut case— fraud, pure-and-simple. And you know what that means?"

"No. What?"

"Triple damages! *Yes-sir-ree*, triple damages."

When confronted with the damaging evidence, Garrity capitulated. The case was settled out of court for $25,000.

Did Garrity's stamps originate in China? Find their way to Hong Kong? Travel to London? Istanbul? Beirut? Had King Farouk ever owned the stamps? Was there an Egyptian named Hagazi, or an Arab prince with a rhinoceros-horn dagger? Who knows?

What is known is that *such is the stuff that dreams are made of.*

HOT WATER

It was bitterly cold the mid-February morning I arrived at the stately Von Isoe mansion. A high brick wall, at least ten feet tall, surrounded the estate, and a massive wrought-iron gate blocked the entryway. Von Isoe's neighborhood was at the very pinnacle of upscale: at the end of a confusingly winding street; a brick wall rather than a fence; abundant landscaping, leafless in the grip of winter; and red United Burglar Alarm Company shields everywhere to warn off intruders.

The brawny young security guard at the front gate confirmed that I had the right address. Walkie-talkie to his lips, he announced my arrival: "Visitor on his way up to the house." He motioned me through. I proceeded slowly up the long, curved driveway, crushed rock crunching under my tires.

A young woman, impeccably and conservatively dressed, greeted me at the front door. She escorted me up a broad flight of stairs to an expansive second floor study. I marveled at the room. It was bright, airy, and sumptuous. Without question, it belonged to a very wealthy man.

Von Isoe had spared no expense furnishing it. Guests were treated to overstuffed leather chairs and sofas so large and comfortable that having sat down, one would almost certainly find it difficult to get up again.

Bookshelves lined the walls. Sculpture and artifacts crowded tables and shelves: classic Greek vases; sea-green jade horses; African tribal figures carved in dark exotic woods; crudely hewn,

colorfully painted Indian totems; and magnificent sea shells—
marvelously large and delicately colored—mounted on marble bases.

On the far side of the study, a smiling man in his early forties rose
and came forward to greet me. "I'm Harold Walker," he said,
extending his right hand.

My visit to the Von Isoe mansion had been set in motion by a
telephone call from Walker a couple of days earlier. "What do you
charge for appraisals?" he had asked.

"Twenty-five dollars an hour at my office, fifty dollars an hour at
your location, or two and a half percent of the appraised value,
whichever is greater. One hour minimum," I replied.

"That works out to five thousand dollars for a two hundred
thousand dollar appraised value, if my math is correct."

"Yes. However, the fee is negotiable on large properties." I added.
Two hundred thousand dollar collections don't come along every
day. I was eager to look at it, and perhaps do business. "Is the
collection for sale?" I asked hopefully. "The fee is waived if we buy
it."

"No, it's not for sale. I'm an insurance agent. I need an appraisal to
verify a casualty loss. It's a rather large collection with extensive
water damage. I need to know whether it's a total or partial loss, the
dollar value of the loss, and the value of the collection in general. The
policyholder is claiming a two hundred thousand dollar loss. Because
of the size of the claim, I need an accurate, reliable written appraisal."

"I never put anything in an appraisal that I wouldn't swear to in a
court of law," I replied.

"All right. How about ten o'clock Thursday morning?"

"Sounds fine," I said.

"Great, I'll see you there," Walker said, then gave me directions to
the Von Isoe estate.

"Glad to meet you," I said, shaking Harold Walker's hand. Mr.
Von Isoe was nowhere in evidence.

"The collection is over here," Walker said, pointing toward a large
conference table covered with Minkus international albums. Their
navy blue covers were warped and discolored. It was obvious they
had gotten wet.

"I'll just take a quick look," I said, "and let you know what I think."

"Fine. Take as much time as you need."

The dozen or so albums contained a great number of stamps, mostly colorful approval sets: pretty, postwar Hungarian cancelled-to-order sets; San Marino short sets—butterflies, dogs and birds; exotic Mozambique pictorials; impressive-looking, but inexpensive, Liechtenstein postage dues; bright, fresh-as-the-day-they-were-printed Latin American Seebecks; Liberian pictorials showcasing a menagerie of wild animals. Unfortunately, for all their bulk, the albums contained little substance. The whole works didn't amount to $1,000.

"May I speak to you for a moment, privately?" I said softly to Walker. Von Isoe's exquisitely dressed, perfectly groomed secretary, mildly curious, looked up discreetly from the oversized mahogany desk where she had busied herself with paperwork. When we reached the far side of the room, our backs to the young woman, I asked, "Is that the entire collection?"

"Yes," he replied, looking puzzled. "Why?"

"The albums are worth more than the stamps."

He drew back his neck in an unconscious gesture of surprise, then frowned and said, "Are you sure?"

"Positive. The stamps are ultra-common. They don't come close to being worth even a thousand dollars, let alone two hundred thousand."

"Are you absolutely sure?" he repeated, still looking puzzled.

Had the same thought crossed our minds simultaneously? *Is Von Isoe trying to pull a fast one?*

"Yes, I'm sure," I said. "Most of the stamps are used. That is, they have no gum on the back, so getting wet hasn't damaged them. They could easily be remounted." Aside from a few mint sets that were stuck down, the main damage appeared to be to the albums. "The only real loss is the ruined albums, maybe six to eight hundred dollars worth."

"I see," Walker said, rubbing his chin thoughtfully. Then, "I want you to make an itemized inventory of every stamp in the collection. Can you do that?"

"Yes, but it's really not worth the expense. The entire collection, albums and all, won't amount to two thousand dollars at the absolute most—and that's stretching it. It'll take hours. At fifty dollars an hour, you're going to spend far more on the appraisal than the stamps are worth."

"I understand," Walker said. "Nevertheless, I'd like to have it done. I want to know the precise value of the entire collection—the value of the damaged stamps, the cost of new albums and hinges, and the cost of labor to remount the collection."

"The cost of labor to remount the collection will be more than the stamps are worth," I cautioned.

"Nevertheless, please calculate the costs as I've outlined. I'll pay your fee."

"Okay," I said, shrugging. Another thing puzzled me. "Where were the stamps kept? How did they get wet?"

"They were stored in the basement in cardboard boxes. Unfortunately, the boxes were underneath a pipe that burst."

A likely story, I thought. Judging by the way Von Isoe's other prized collectibles were displayed in his museum-like study, it didn't sound plausible that he would store an enormously valuable stamp collection in cardboard boxes in his basement.

"Can you start right away. I'd like to settle this claim as quickly as possible. You have my number. Give me a call when you get back to your office. One more thing, this matter is strictly confidential. Don't discuss your findings with anyone except me. Understood?"

I nodded.

"Good luck," he said. He shook my hand and departed.

As I slowly worked my way through the albums, noting catalogue values and numbers, I thought, *how ironic*. After all my years in the business, with all my knowledge and experience, here I am in a three-piece suit, in the home of a wealthy businessman, toting up approval stamps, the very same issues I eagerly collected as a ten-year-old. And being paid fifty dollars an hour to do it.

Only the metronomic ticking of an antique grandfather clock on the far side of the room intruded on the silence. The chicly dressed, fashion-model secretary continued to work quietly on her files and papers. At noon, she buzzed for the security guard.

"I'm taking a lunch break," she said, "Arnold will stay with you until I get back."

"Fine," I said. "I'd prefer not be left alone with the stamps." Of course, they had no way of knowing the stamps were packet material.

As far as they knew, the collection was worth $200,000. I plodded on, inventorying basically worthless stamps, watched over by a beefy security guard.

At one o'clock, the young woman returned to her desk, and the security guard left. By two o'clock the sheer mindlessness of the task, together with the rhythmic tick-tock of the grandfather clock, had nearly lulled me to sleep. I fought the irresistible urge to put my head on the table and nap. By three o'clock I felt as if I had been without sleep for 24 hours. Time slowed to a crawl. It took great effort just to concentrate. The task became increasingly boring. Column after column filled with repetitive figures—10 cents, 15 cents, 25 cents, and, occasionally even 50 cents or a dollar.

Nevertheless, I was determined to finish by the end of the day. The last thing I wanted was to have to return the next day. By four o'clock I was ready to lose my mind. It occurred to me that being forced to itemize worthless stamps could be employed as a form of psychological torture. When five o'clock finally arrived, I had finished. My back and shoulders ached from sitting too long. When I stood, I could barely straighten up. My whole body felt like one gigantic cramp. I left, vowing never to undertake that kind of appraisal again, regardless of how well it paid.

After I had formalized my notes the following morning, I called Harold Walker. "Looks like you could replace the albums and the stamps that were actually damaged and remount the collection for about sixteen hundred dollars. It breaks down like this: three hundred fifty dollars—which is liberal—to replace the stamps, seven hundred fifty dollars to replace the albums, and five hundred dollars to remount the collection. The appraisal fee comes to three hundred fifty dollars. I almost feel guilty charging you that much, the collection is so marginal."

"I'm happy to pay it," Walker replied. "It sure beats having to pay a claim of two hundred thousand dollars."

I hadn't thought of it that way, but he had a point. I'd just saved him more than $198,000.

"Do you think Von Isoe was trying to beat you out of two hundred thousand bucks?" I asked. "Anyone who knows anything about stamps would know the collection is worth very little." The question was born of cynicism, and no sooner had I said it than I was sorry. I should have kept my mouth shut. It wasn't my place to question.

Still, the claim smacked of insurance fraud. Had I been Walker, I would have been mad as hell.

"The thought crossed my mind," he said, "but Von Isoe claims he took the collection from a friend as collateral for a personal loan. His friend told him the collection was quite valuable, worth at least the two hundred thousand dollars that Von Isoe lent him. Based on that, Von Isoe insured the collection with us for two hundred thousand."

"Some friend," I remarked. It still smelled fishy to me, and I couldn't hide my skepticism. "And you think he's on the level?"

"I have no reason to doubt him. He's been paying rather hefty premiums for the two hundred thousand dollar coverage. He says he's not a stamp collector, knows nothing about stamps, and isn't the slightest bit interested in them. Mr. Von Isoe is in the oil business. His corporation buys a lot of insurance from us. The annual premiums are substantial, far in excess of two hundred thousand dollars. He's a valued customer. This claim turned out to be trivial, so I'm not about to suggest that anything improper might have occurred. I just want to get the claim settled. After all, it's not our fault that his friend stuck him with a worthless collection. I *am* going to suggest that he have all his property appraised, for his benefit as well as ours.

"Well, I've got to run," Walker said. "Thanks for your help. Send the appraisal and your bill. I'll get a check out to you right away."

After hearing Harold Walker's remarks, I felt a little foolish about my suspicions. Perhaps I shouldn't have jumped to conclusions.

It is entirely possible that Von Isoe stored the collection in boxes because it was something to be left intact until reclaimed.

On the other hand, a basement is an odd place to keep something so valuable.

But then, Von Isoe had no way of knowing the pipe would burst . . . *did he?*

I guess we'll never know.

TOO GOOD TO BE TRUE

"What do you think of this stamp?" the doctor said, using long narrow tongs to carefully remove a vividly colored blue duck stamp from its mount. He handed me both stamp and tongs.

The stamp was magnificent. Ridges of deep sapphire-colored intaglio ink rose, like miniature mountain ranges, above the stamp's pure Arctic-white paper. The contrast was striking, the blue and the white equally bright, equally vivid. The Mallards seemed ready to fly right off the surface of the paper. And if that weren't enough, oversized, perfectly symmetrical borders framed the design. I held in my hands the most superb example of Scott No. RW1, the first federal duck hunting stamp, I had ever seen.

The doctor waited expectantly for my opinion. The stamp was absolutely perfect—too perfect.

"It's been regummed," I announced. "Beautifully done, too. An expert job by a real craftsman."

"Oh?" the doctor murmured, neither as surprised nor disappointed as I'd expected. "Are you sure?"

"Yes."

"Absolutely sure?" he persisted.

I wouldn't have offered the opinion if I hadn't been sure. I wondered how he would react to a patient who questioned his diagnosis. Would he be mildly annoyed?

"For one thing," I said, "the gum is much whiter that it should be." His expression remained skeptical, as if to say, "The gum looks perfectly fine to me. How do you know it's too white?" The man needed convincing.

"The stamp was printed in the 1930s by flat plate press. Let's compare its gum with genuine examples of that era." I extracted an inexpensive, never-hinged stamp from a stock book and laid it atop the duck stamp. The commemorative's gum was straw colored, appeared almost dingy compared to the bright, transparent whiteness of the duck stamp's gum. "See the difference?" I asked.

The doctor studied the two stamps, turning and shifting them in the light. "There is a difference," he admitted. "But it's possible that different gums were used."

"Not likely," I said. "The Bureau of Engraving and Printing didn't stock special gums for each stamp. They used the same basic gum for all stamp production. And they used the same production process for all stamps—lock plates onto press, fill ink fountain, print stamps, apply gum, and perforate. Ducks, commems, definitives or whatever, were all done the same.

"The point is, gums of that era all look fairly similar. I could pull a dozen examples to prove the point. The gum on your stamp is far too white and transparent. It just doesn't look right," I said emphatically. I wasn't used to having my opinion questioned, especially by an amateur. Perhaps I took umbrage where no offense was intended.

"I was afraid it might be regummed," the doctor said with a sigh. "I'm a serious collector. I'm getting to the point of having to spend serious money to fill blank spaces, so I'm just trying to learn more about the dangers of doctored stamps. I think I've been taken. Remember last fall, I asked you about my number three and number four?" He was referring to Scott Nos. 3 and 4, official reproductions of the first U.S. postage stamps. I recalled the incident, recalled telling him that his stamps looked like proofs. Proofs of Scott Nos. 3 and 4 are worth considerably less than the actual stamps.

"I remember," I said.

"I got the duck stamp from the same guy."

"Ah, well then, no surprise it's regummed. Let me give you a few pointers. The stamp looks too good, too perfect. When you've seen as many stamps as I have, you instinctively become suspicious of anything as perfect as your duck stamp. It's hard to explain in purely objective terms. I think it all boils down to experience. When you've seen enough stamps, you know what good ones look like and what bad ones look like. And right at first glance, your stamp didn't look right to me.

"First off, it's too bright and too fresh. Both the paper and the gum are too white. Compare them with other ducks of the 1930s right there on your album page." The RW1's paper blazed snow-white. The other duck stamps' paper appeared somewhat yellowish, even dingy by comparison.

"Your stamp's so bright you almost need sunglasses to look at it. It's been bleached, then regummed. It may have been bleached to remove a washable blue signature, or simply to remove the natural dinginess of age. Whoever did it was a real craftsman. Most bleachers leave stamps in too long, and color suffers as a result. But your stamp literally blazes. And look at the way the gum was applied. The texture is beautiful, nearly perfect . . . but not quite one hundred percent authentic. It's good enough to fool the unpracticed eye, though, especially when it's sitting all by itself on a stock sheet. Your duck stamp was reconditioned by a highly skilled stamp mechanic, an A-number-one expert.

"Now feel the perforation teeth," I said. "The ends are hard and rigid." I showed him how to pull his finger lightly across the edges of the stamp. "Compare that to the feel of an unaltered stamp." I handed him a genuine stamp for comparison. "The rigidity, the relative hardness is caused by the still-liquid gum ever so slightly soaking into the perf-ends during regumming. The hardening effect is almost impossible to prevent. It's the first thing to look for when you suspect regumming. The hardening on your stamp is minimal. Nevertheless, it's there.

"No question, the stamp is beautiful. It screams to be owned. However, to the experienced eye, perfection signals danger. Experience teaches one to beware of inordinately perfect stamps."

"I see what you mean," the doctor said. He looked discouraged, but at least he'd begun to understand the pitfalls of altered stamps and the importance of knowledge.

"It happens all the time," I said, trying to console him. "I took a consignment for auction last year from a businessman who had purchased only superb mint U.S. stamps. He had lots of late nineteenth century material—banknotes, Columbians, first Bureau issues, etc., mostly complete sets. The stamps were gorgeous, every one visually stunning, fresh-as-the-day-they-were-printed, crisply-colored, large-margined gems. And every one reconditioned—regummed, regummed over thins, reperfed, rebacked, you name it.

" 'Auction them off,' he told me. 'I'm through with stamps. I paid premium prices for every one. Trusted the dealer completely. Thought he was the greatest. Then, when I sent the high values for Philatelic Foundation certificates, I learned that every single stamp had been altered. I spent thousands with the guy. I'm just sick over the whole business.'

"The businessman's voice was subdued, heavy with disappointment. As he spoke, I glanced at the certificates. Their verdicts, eloquent in their simplicity: *Genuine but regummed over a filled thin. Genuine but reperforated at right. Genuine but regummed and reperforated at bottom.* Not an unaltered stamp in the bunch.

" 'While I was buying,' the businessman said, 'the question of genuineness never occurred to me. As far as I was concerned, the certificates were simply icing on the cake. I was shocked to learn that every single stamp had been altered. I was cheated, plain and simple. What a fool I've been!'

" 'Sell them all,' he told me, heaving a sigh. 'I never want to see them again.'

"You're aware that I'll have to describe your stamps honestly in my auction," I advised him. "I'll have to mention that they're regummed, reperfed, etc. And described as such, they'll only realize about ten to twenty percent of catalogue.

" 'I don't care,' he said. 'Just sell them. I'll be satisfied with whatever I get. I never want to see another stamp as long as I live.'

"You don't need to be an expert to spot glaring inconsistencies," I told the doctor, hoping the hobby was not about to lose another collector. "All you need is awareness.

"To demonstrate this point to the businessman, I turned all his Columbians gum side up. With the exception of a couple of low values, none of the gums matched. There were gray gums, yellow gums, white gums, smooth gums, rough gums—no two the same. Doesn't it strike you as odd that every single stamp in the series would have such markedly different gum?" I asked the doctor. He nodded in agreement.

"Then, I put them under ultraviolet light. The differences were glaringly evident. Some fluoresced brightly, others not at all, and, again, with the exception of the untampered low values, each fluoresced differently. Without question, the stamps had been altered.

You don't have to be an expert to notice such blatantly obvious differences.

"Certain stamps—especially nineteenth century issues—are prone to regumming and reperfing. It's prudent to regard all such never-hinged stamps with caution. That doesn't mean that every stamp has been 'reconditioned,' only that the likelihood is great, so one should be cautious. It's best not to give a stamp the benefit of the doubt until you have examined it carefully. At the same time, don't let paranoia spoil your enjoyment of the hobby. Simply be prudent, develop a healthy sense of skepticism."

"I was taken," the doctor sighed. "I should have known better. I shop the classified ads of the daily paper for stamps for sale. You can make some real buys that way.

"A classified ad appeared a while back, placed by a man who was privately liquidating his better U.S. stamps. When I called, I got an answering service. The service took my number and told me the man would call me back. Soon after, he did. He was a pleasant fellow, sounded nice on the phone. He told me he was retired, and the time had come to sell some of his better pieces. He suggested that we meet in the lobby of a local hotel. He said he had been in the hotel business and felt comfortable doing business in hotels. I thought perhaps he was just being cautious. You never know who you're going to meet through the classified ads, so I assumed he wanted to keep his residence address private. His suggestion didn't strike me as terribly unusual or unreasonable.

"We met at the hotel. He took me to a quiet spot with a table where we could do business. I was dazzled the moment he opened his stock book." The doctor's eyes widened, and, at the same time, he spread his hands outward from his face in sunburst fashion to emphasize his amazement. "The stamps were gorgeous, every single, solitary item!"

"You should have been suspicious right then," I said.

"I should have been, but I was completely awed by the quality of the stamps. I'd never met anyone who had such a pristine stock of U.S. mint stamps."

I didn't interrupt to explain that the reason he had never seen such a pristine stock of early mint stamps is because they don't exist, at least not in a legitimate, unaltered state.

"I was so impressed I wanted to buy them all," the doctor said. "I even called my accountant to see if I could raid my pension plan. Thank God, he said no. So I settled for a few.

"I bought the duck stamp, the Scott Nos. 3 and 4, and a couple other items. Spent about fifteen hundred dollars. The seller insisted on being paid in cash. That seemed okay, too. After all, he didn't know me. I thought he was just being prudent. I wish I had been.

"Later, I became suspicious. Especially after your remarks last fall about the Nos. 3 and 4. I decided to find out his address. All I had to go on was his phone number at the answering service. Fortunately, I happened to know a fellow doctor who had an office in the same building as the answering service. I explained what happened. As luck would have it, he knew the woman who owned the answering service. He told me to call her, use his name as a reference, and see if she could help. She was just great, very cooperative. My story intrigued her, so she gave me the man's address. Turns out, he lives in Texas. He wasn't even from Denver."

"Doesn't it strike you as strange that a man from Texas would advertise in Denver papers to sell his collection?" I asked.

"It does now, but at the time I didn't know he lived in Texas," the doctor said.

Stamps too good to be true, prices too good to be true, and oddly incongruous circumstances all should arouse suspicion. A seller accessible only through an answering service, whose real telephone number you never know, whose address you never know, who's willing to meet you only in a hotel, whose stock is uniformly superlative, who insists on being paid in cash, when taken together, should stop you cold, like a highway flagman jumping up and down, frantically waving a red flag in each hand.

The doctor was lucky. He escaped without blowing his life's savings. In how many other cities has the phantom retiree placed classified ads, hired answering services, set up meetings in hotels, displayed outrageously superb—albeit doctored—material, been paid in cash, then vanished? Who knows?

Be careful! He may still be out there.

PART THREE

MEMORABLE CHARACTERS

THEY MIGHT BE GIANTS

It began with a letter whose language reached for eloquence, perhaps a bit too hard.

"Greetings," the letter began, "I want to wish you and your illustrious firm a prosperous new year."

It was handwritten, the script decorated with elaborate serifs. The penmanship, doubtlessly intended as elegant calligraphy, came across as an ornate scrawl. The lines sloped upward and bunched together, as handwritten lines are prone to do on unruled paper.

The writer went on to assure me that he would recommend me to all his friends because of my courtesy in our past business affairs. That struck me as odd because I had never heard of him before.

Karl Henry Pfalzgraf III, the author of the letter, wanted to dispose of several volumes of autographs and stamps. The list of autographs read like *Who's Who in European Royalty*: the Grand Duke, the Grand Duchess and the Princess of Luxembourg; Prince Franz Joseph II, Prince Hans-Adam, Prince Michael, and Princess Gina; Princess Grace of Monaco; President Valery Giscard D'Estang; and Pope Paul II, to name a few. Although the letter focused on royal autographs, it also mentioned stamps. That raised my interest level a notch because the autographs, despite their glamour, were worth little on the market.

It sounded like Pfalzgraf had gone to a lot of trouble to obtain the autographs. So, I reasoned, they might be the icing on good foundation collections of useful countries such as Luxembourg, Liechtenstein, and Monaco.

The letter gave no clue to the scope or value of the collection. Normally, I would have called Karl Henry Pfalzgraf III to learn more about it, but the letter lacked a telephone number. I tried information, but they had no listing for the man. The omission of a phone number didn't strike me as unusual because more than half the letters inquiring about selling collections lack a phone number. The return address was a post office box. That, too, wasn't unusual, since collectors often use boxes to protect their privacy.

Karl Henry Pfalzgraf III stated that it wouldn't be possible for him to get to Loveland, Colorado, where I operated my business; could I come to Denver to view the collection? He suggested that we meet at the Denver Public Library. In fact, he was rather adamant about it.

"They have excellent facilities for viewing collections such as mine," his letter stated. The comment also struck me as odd. I was completely familiar the Denver Public Library, but unaware of any special stamp viewing facilities.

The letter was boldly signed, the name underscored by a sweeping flourish.

I read it over a couple of times. I wasn't sure whether to take it seriously or not. I guess it was the last sentence that intrigued me: "I promise that you will be delighted with the collection!"

Dealers learn to size up letters—and sellers—quickly. In the course of a career, you develop a healthy amount of cynicism, having heard far too many claims about wonderful collections. Every seller, it seems, claims to have a wonderful collection, just as every parent has bright, gifted children, and every job applicant is hard-working and reliable. The tendency of sellers to over-describe their collections has prompted one dealer acquaintance of mine to set forth his own First Law of Philately: *Sellers always lie.* And he stands by it adamantly. In my opinion, that statement is a little strong. Still, sellers do tend to exaggerate. I don't think they mean to. It's just natural to be proud of your property.

Was Pfalzgraf exaggerating? My better judgment told me yes: *Don't be a fool! Don't waste a trip.* My spirit of adventure disagreed and nagged: *Go ahead, meet Pfalzgraf! Look at the collection. What do you have to lose?*

Curiosity won out. Against my better judgment, I wrote Karl Henry Pfalzgraf III and agreed to meet him at the library in Denver.

January weather in Colorado is always unpredictable. The morning I made the 55-mile drive from Loveland to Denver was no exception. It had all the earmarks of a bad day. Low gunmetal-gray overcast barely cleared the tops of downtown skyscrapers. The air was dense, moist, and frigid. It smelled of snow. More than a foot of snow from a previous storm still covered the city, although the streets had been plowed and were passable. I was anxious meet to Karl Henry Pfalzgraf III, conclude our business, and get back on the road to Loveland. I didn't want to be caught on the interstate if it started to snow in earnest. High-plains whiteouts are terrifying and deadly. More than one traveler has been discovered frozen to death after a winter storm.

I arrived early at the Denver Public Library for our ten o'clock meeting. I paced the floor near the main entrance, waiting for Karl Henry Pfalzgraf III to appear. At ten minutes past ten, I began to wonder whether he was going to show up or whether I had wasted a trip. Ten more minutes, I said to myself. I'll give him ten more minutes and then I'm gone. I watched and waited. Occasional, almost weightless flecks of snow floated ever so slowly to the ground. From my vantage point behind floor-to-ceiling plate glass windows near the library's front entrance, the world looked very bleak and cold. Pedestrians, bundled up against the Arctic air, traversed the sparse, frozen, white landscape like figures from a Brueghel winter scene.

At a quarter past ten, a southbound Broadway bus materialized out of the gloom. It stopped just north of Fourteenth Avenue and deposited a passenger laden with three-ring binders. Then it groaned wearily into motion, belching black smoke into the low overcast. As it pulled away, Karl Henry Pfalzgraf III trudged across Fourteenth Avenue toward the library. He was bundled up against the cold in a nondescript dark overcoat. A long, checkered muffler, which once-upon-a-time had been brightly colored, coiled around his neck and up over his chin like an exhausted, dispirited boa. A knit ski cap pulled down over his ears completed the outfit. Burdened with albums, he made his way slowly toward the library's entrance.

"Mr. Pfalzgraf?" I asked, as he came through the front door.

"Why, yes," he replied, "And, of course, you must be Mr. Datz." He sounded genuinely pleased to meet me. "There's an excellent table toward the rear that will afford us a good degree of privacy, and it's near the windows so we can take advantage of this fine morning light."

"Can I help you with the albums?"

"Why, thank you." he said. I took several off the top and followed him to the viewing table.

Karl Henry Pfalzgraf III set the albums carefully on the table, then turned and extended his hand. "It is, indeed, a great pleasure to meet you," he said, pumping my hand enthusiastically.

"It's nice to meet you, too," I replied.

He unwrapped his muffler, then removed his coat, placing it carefully, almost ceremoniously, on the back of a chair. Without his coat, Karl Henry Pfalzgraf looked thin and gaunt. His clothes had seen better days, but brightness blazed in his eyes and cheeriness warmed his words. It struck me that the sheer force of these qualities alone gave form and substance to Karl Henry Pfalzgraf III.

"You will have no reason to be disappointed in my collection," he said. I hoped he was right, but years of experience had taught me never to set my expectations too high.

He set about arranging his albums as he spoke. It makes little difference to a stamp dealer in what order albums are viewed. Value isn't a function of arrangement. Nevertheless, sellers often consider it important to present a collection in its logical sequence, an etiquette I never disrespect.

"The Liechtenstein, Luxembourg, and Monaco collections contain royal covers, cacheted first day covers, and autographed portraits of Princess Grace, Grand Duke Jean and Grand Duchess Charlotte, and many others," Pfalzgraf said.

I got the impression from the reverent solemnity in his voice that I was about to be introduced to them in person. At the same time, I hoped to see an abundance of good stamps from Liechtenstein, Luxembourg, and Monaco. I listened politely, nodding now and then, all the while anxious to get started, to see what Karl Henry Pfalzgraf III's albums contained.

"I will accept in good faith any offer you quote," he said, finishing the arrangement. The remark took me off guard. I was used to negotiating with sellers who, more often than not, had unrealistically high opinions of their collections' values and were prepared to fight tooth and nail to get every last cent. Accustomed to that kind of negotiation, I felt a sudden burden of responsibility to quote a liberal price to this enigmatic person whose sense of business etiquette was so out of the ordinary. Karl Henry Pfalzgraf's remark implied that his approach was the only honorable way in which gentlemen conduct business.

I opened the first album expecting to see pages full of glorious mint sets. Instead, I found lots of postcards, notes, FDCs, and photos. I turned a few pages, still hoping. Occasionally, a stray stamp graced a page, but not often. There were lots of autographed notes, cards, and photos, but stamps were few and far between. That sinking feeling known to every stamp dealer who has ever gone on a wild-goose chase began to grip me. Without going any further, I knew the stamps wouldn't amount to much.

I was about to reach for the next album when Karl Henry Pfalzgraf III directed my attention back to the one I'd just finished. He opened it again and patiently began explaining the contents, as if I'd whisked through it too quickly.

"I exchange cards with the royal families every year," he said, as if they were personal friends. I listened and nodded politely, unsure whether I was surprised, amused, or simply dumbfounded. "Ah, yes, here is an announcement of the wedding of Prince Henri and Maria Teresa."

I had no idea who Prince Henri or Maria Teresa were. I didn't want to reveal my ignorance, so I just muttered, "Mmm, very nice."

"And here's a note thanking me for my wedding gift." The note was neatly handwritten in English on expensive stationery. Embossed in gold, the royal coat of arms stood out elegantly at the top of the sheet.

He sent them a wedding gift? I thought to myself. *And they sent him a thank you note?*

"The gift was nothing much, but then we've never met. I've only corresponded with their parents," he explained.

Did that remark mean he had met neither the parents nor the youngsters, or that he had met the parents but not the youngsters? He spoke as if the correspondents were personal friends; at least his tone implied as much. Or was I misinterpreting what he said?

"And here's a thank you note for my congratulations to Grand Duke Jean and Grand Duchess Josephine Charlotte on the occasion of their silver wedding anniversary." Indeed, it was. The handwritten note in English read, "Dear Karl, Thank you for remembering our anniversary with your kind note of March 25th. I hope you and your family are well."

Then, a thought struck me like a thunderbolt: *What if he really does know all these celebrities!*

Karl Henry Pfalzgraf III guided me from album to album, introducing me to all his friends as we went. "Here's a note from Prince Rainier," he said. "Princess Grace's death was such a horrible tragedy. She was such a fine lady." The genuine sense of loss in his voice, again, made me wonder if he had known her personally. Page after page, birthday greetings, Christmas greetings, and personal notes paraded onward, the royal procession guided by a proud Karl Henry Pfalzgraf and observed by a slightly bewildered stamp dealer.

The postcards, FDCs, and notes were of little commercial value, but Pfalzgraf's comments and stories increasingly intrigued me. Who was this frail, curious gentleman? Why should European royalty remember his birthdays, send him greetings and personal notes? Why was he dressed in hand-me-down clothes?

Album followed album. The volume of autographed correspondence was impressive, but the precious few stamps catalogued next to nothing. The collection was not at all what I had expected. Still, Karl Henry Pfalzgraf III fascinated me so much that I forgot how disappointed I was in the collection.

I kept wondering if he actually knew European royalty. Or had he constructed an elaborate fantasy, a fantasy in which he—a kindred spirit—corresponded with nobility as if he were almost, but not quite, one of them? He was a courteous man, well spoken and, seemingly, well educated. I got the impression that he spent many hours writing kind, thoughtful letters to personalities who inhabited a world in which he would like to have lived. It was a world of high protocol and gentility; a world peopled by dukes and duchesses, barons, counts, and earls, where stellar among them reigned kings and queens, princes and grand dukes; a world of fancy dress balls and state dinners; a world far from the humble reality of his station in life. The albums, the correspondence, and Karl Henry Pfalzgraf III himself led me to my conclusion.

I thought, So what, if it seems odd? What harm is there in it? The English treasure their eccentrics almost as much as they treasure their royalty. Who am I to judge?

Karl Henry Pfalzgraf III apparently had no telephone. His address was a post office box. His clothes were far past prime. His collection was mounted in dime store photo albums. Yet it contained a large body of personal correspondence from a variety of royal personalities. Why did he want to sell it? I could only assume he needed money. There could be no other explanation, since the collection clearly meant a lot to him.

I could have asked him how he met the princes and princesses, but I chose not to. The question almost certainly would have embarrassed him, and I didn't want to do that.

As Karl Henry Pfalzgraf III guided me through his collection, I drew some conclusions. I deduced that he had gotten to know the royal personalities because he had written them often. He had written to them on their birthdays, on their anniversaries, on the weddings of the children, on the deaths of family members, at Christmas and Easter, and on any other occasion that seemed appropriate. He was gently persistent. He wrote in his own pseudo-formal, flowery, pretentious language, the kind he imagined they used in everyday conversation. He wished them well. And he was sincere.

Even though I had just met him, I concluded that they had responded to the genuine kindness in his letters. And suddenly I felt it important to respect the strange protocol that seemed to govern the eccentric world of Karl Henry Pfalzgraf.

In the movie *They Might Be Giants*, George C. Scott played a character who thought he was Sherlock Holmes. He spent his time on the trail of arch-villain Professor Moriarty. Scott's brother, convinced that he was completely out of touch with reality, arranged to have him examined by a psychiatrist who, coincidentally, happened to be named Dr. Elizabeth Watson. As far as Scott was concerned, Elizabeth was his long-lost assistant, the real Dr. Watson. He explained his suspicions of Moriarty's latest evil enterprise to her, then dragged her along on his quest to find the villain and solve the mystery. The funny thing is, as the film progressed, Dr. Watson began to sympathize with Scott, perhaps even believe him. The movie left the viewer up in the air, thinking that perhaps Scott's world may not have been entirely imaginary.

"Well, what do you think?" Karl Henry Pfalzgraf III asked when we had finished the last album.

"It's very nice," I replied. "But I'm sure its sentimental value is worth far more than its market value." I had grown to like Karl Henry. His courtesy and civility impressed me. I wanted to let him down easily, diplomatically. I had no idea of how much he thought the collection was worth, and I was afraid to ask. I imagined figures such as $1,000, $2,500, or even $5,000. Unfortunately, I estimated the collection's real value to be about $50—maximum.

"Well, as I previously stated, any offer you quote will be accepted in good faith."

I cringed. "Perhaps you ought to keep it," I said. "I don't think I could offer you anywhere near what you feel it's worth."

"Well, it's something I've enjoyed, but to be frank, I could use the money. The time has come to let someone else enjoy it as much as I have." He looked me straight in the eye, and I knew instantly that Karl Henry Pfalzgraf III really did need the money, perhaps desperately. I also realized that it would embarrass him to talk about it further.

"As I said, the autographs really aren't worth much. There's little demand for them, but let me see what I can do." I paged through the albums once again to confirm my initial estimate. "Fifty dollars is the best I can do," I said, hating to offer so little.

"That will be acceptable." He didn't flinch at all. "Of course, I had hoped for more, but I will abide by your professional appraisal." He looked straight at me, chin up, eyes clear and bright. His thin, wan face didn't reveal the slightest disappointment in having to part with his treasure.

I wrote out a check and handed it to him. "I wish it could be for more," I said apologetically.

"I'm sure you treated me more than fairly," he replied.

"Can I give you a lift?"

"I would appreciate that very much. Here, let me help you with those albums," he said, rising and putting on his coat.

The overcast spit light snow as we left the library and headed west along Fourteenth Avenue toward my car. We crossed Acoma and passed in front of the Denver Art Museum. It loomed above us, a modern gray granite castle, its syncopated crenellations nearly lost in the low hanging overcast. It brought to mind images of castles on the Rhine and knights of old. *Perhaps Karl Henry Pfalzgraf III is descended from a long and noble line*, I thought. *Perhaps he's just down on his luck. Perhaps. Perhaps. Perhaps.*

"Where to?" I asked.

"Do you know where the Nineteenth Street viaduct is?"

"Yes."

"Just drop me off on the far side of the viaduct. It's right near the freeway entrance, very convenient for your journey north."

"I'd be glad to take you all the way—"

"No, no, that's really not necessary. No need to put you out of your way." His tone was firm and insistent. He was a considerate man. Or perhaps he didn't want me to take him all the way home. Perhaps he didn't have a permanent home. Perhaps he lived in a faceless tenement. Perhaps he didn't want me to see where he lived. I'll never know, because I didn't press the issue. I dropped him on the far side of the viaduct.

"Thank you very much for your courtesy, Mr. Datz," he said. "I wish you well."

He waved as I pulled away from the curb. Snow swirled more heavily now, and when I glanced in my rearview mirror for one last look at Karl Henry Pfalzgraf III, he was gone, dematerialized in the dense flurry of whiteness that had been waiting all morning to fall. It was as if he had never existed at all.

Months later, the Pfalzgraf correspondence appeared in one of my auctions. It realized $40.

FAST EDDIE

They're known by many names: mystery lots, job lots, junk lots, remainders, and in Eddie's case, grot lots. And they have a devoted following. Perhaps it's the lure of hidden treasure or the simple pleasure of sorting through thousands and thousands of stamps. Whatever the reason, plenty of collectors like mystery lots, and Eddie couldn't get enough of them.

Mystery lots are born in stamp dealers' back rooms. They begin as cardboard cartons into which all sorts of stray stamps and covers find their way, sometimes even complete albums and stock books. They receive the odds and ends that dealers have neither the time nor patience to sort and identify: non-Scott-listed stamps, kiloware, packets, covers, every sort of miscellany.

Are treasures to be found in mystery lots? Of course. Collectors assume—incorrectly—that dealers know every stamp, or at least recognize all the rare ones. It's just not so. Few, if any, dealers possess completely comprehensive knowledge. Collectors also incorrectly assume that dealers check every last stamp that passes through their hands. Again, it's just not so.

From a dealer's standpoint, it's uneconomical to spend hours, or pay someone to spend hours, sifting accumulations for elusive rarities.

Of course, I'm speaking as a dealer, not a collector. There are things one does for fun that he wouldn't do for a living. Spending long blissful hours with a mystery lot is one of them. Hoping to find the pot of gold, the megabuck rarity, is part of the hobby's allure.

As a dealer, my business philosophy is to toss bulging, age-browned glassines stuffed with potential rarities into budding mystery lots and let the next fellow find the treasure. If he finds a valuable rarity, so much the better. Word spreads, and you can't buy better advertising.

During the years I maintained an office in Denver, cartons filled up at the rate of two or three a week. And, that's how I came to know Eddie.

"I'm here to buy some stamps," Eddie announced on his first visit. My receptionist, Debbie, looked him up and down and must have harbored some doubts as she buzzed me. Wearing a once-upon-a-time-bright plaid shirt, over-the-hill blue jeans, a well-worn, olive-drab military fatigue jacket, and black work boots, Eddie had obviously not read *Dress for Success.*

"There's a man here to see you," she said. Debbie and I had a code. If she announced a person by name, it indicated that she thought I probably would prefer to see him in my office. If she didn't use his name, it indicated that I should come to the reception area.

"I'd like to see what you've got in job lots," Eddie said. Eddie stood about five feet, six inches. He was stocky but not fat, fiftyish, with an impish sort of face that looked freshly scrubbed, bright and sunny. His graying crewcut hair stood crisply at attention. I decided that Eddie had likely been in the military at one time. It wasn't hard to imagine him snapping a salute.

Eddie's smile radiated friendliness. And so it was, in that fleeting moment of first impression, that Eddie's smile outweighed his dingy wardrobe, and I said, "Okay, come on back."

Eddie followed me back to the workroom. I plunked a couple of cartons on the conference table and said, "This one's forty dollars. That one's seventy-five." Eddie plowed right in, rooting around, pulling items from the bottom, the middle and everywhere in between, making a lot of noise and enjoying himself immensely.

Job lot buyers like to go directly to the bottom of a carton to see if there's anything worthwhile there. They believe that mystery lots are "salted" with desirable bait on top, where it will be immediately noticed. That belief is widely held, seemingly one of the unwritten rules of mystery lots.

I'm not suggesting that some dealers don't salt their lots. They do. In fact, I know one dealer who takes great delight in placing goodies at the bottom of his lots, where he knows buyers will look first. He once remarked to me, "One goody on top and one on the bottom— then both bases are covered." His remark still brings a smile to my face. Who's got time to organize mystery lots?

Eddie finished, scooped up all the loose stamps and glassines that had fallen on the table during his indelicate inspection, and dropped them back into the carton.

"Not bad," he said. "They might do." He scrunched his brow into a thoughtful frown and rubbed his chin. "Any break on price if I take 'em both?"

"Sure. Both for a hundred and five dollars."

"Boy, I was hoping you could do better than that. They're nice, but the price seems a little stiff," he said. Still frowning, Eddie perfunctorily riffled through the tops of the cartons as if searching for something to justify the asking price. I remained silent, watching, wondering what he would say next. After a moment, as if it were a great concession on his part, he said, "Make it an even hundred bucks, and you've got yourself a deal."

"Done."

"You're a real gentleman," Eddie said, extending his hand. "A fine man to do business with." He pulled out an old, beat-up wallet from a front pants pocket and carefully extracted $100 in assorted fives, tens, and twenties, carefully keeping the currency pocket tilted away so I couldn't see how much cash it contained.

"You can use the dolly to take the boxes down to your car," I offered.

"That's okay, I don't have a car. Came over on the bus and I'm going back the same way." How Eddie planned to manhandle the cartons onto the bus, I had no idea. At first, the notion of the bus struck me as odd, then somehow it seemed to fit Eddie.

"How often do you get mystery lots, anyway?" he asked.

"We usually have something every week."

"Great! I'll see you next week." And with that, Eddie left, brimming with energy and confidence, newfound treasures in hand.

Over the months, Eddie became a regular. Only occasionally did he miss a week, usually because of a visit to the VA hospital.

"Those darn doctors like to poke around on me," he'd say. But he was never specific about what ailed him, and I never inquired beyond what he volunteered.

We got to know and like Eddie. He would come in rumpled, like a downscale Columbo, and rummage through our mystery lots. His wardrobe was predictable, although at times a little preposterous. On one occasion, in the dead of winter, he showed up wearing an oversized, brightly flowered Hawaiian shirt.

He invariably bought whatever mystery lots we had on hand, but only after perfunctory negotiation.

"How much?"

"Fifty dollars."

"Ouch! You got some gold stashed in there somewhere? Jeez, I must have missed it."

I'd chuckle inwardly and smile outwardly because it was all a sham. Eddie knew I'd make a price concession. Haggling was a ritual.

"Okay, Eddie, forty bucks."

"Done. Boy, I hope I'm not going to end up buried in this one."

"C'mon Eddie, have you ever made a bad buy here?"

Eddie would answer with his big, bright, ingratiating smile. Then, looking at his watch, he'd say, "Gotta run, the chauffeur's waiting." That meant his bus was due at the corner in a few minutes.

Over the months, we learned bits and pieces about Eddie, but the clues were vague. He'd been in the military, had served in Korea, or been stationed in the Far East just after Korea. He lived in a small, older apartment on the south end of downtown Denver, a section of town whose glory days had passed decades earlier. He subsisted on a disability pension that, judging by his clothes and address, couldn't have been much.

He never complained about anything. He remained ever cheerful and optimistic, even though his life was no bowl of cherries. We didn't feel sorry for him, but got the impression that he depended on our mystery lots to make life a little easier. From that impression there arose a vague sense of obligation to have something for him every week. We tried to keep the price of mystery lots in line with his budget—$25 to $100.

Eddie always had a joke or two for us, usually slightly off-color, the fairly harmless kind that might have raised eyebrows twenty years earlier, but now were barely risqué. We laughed, more amused by their corniness than by their humor.

"Didja hear the one about the girl who got lost in the marine barracks?" Eddie would ask. And even though we had, we'd listen to the joke again, piping in with the punch line. Eddie didn't mind having his punch lines preempted. Whenever it happened, we'd all laugh heartily, not at the joke, but good-naturedly at the predictable silliness of the routine.

Eddie's favorite remark, which he invariably made after a deal had been closed and he was ready to leave, was, "Like the girls in Singapore used to say, 'It's been a business doing pleasure with ya.' " He was inordinately fond of it. It became his signature. He'd render it after every deal with a great big impish grin of self-delight. Tom Savoie, who worked for me at the time, and I laughed every time we heard it. We laughed because we knew it was coming, and because we knew Eddie took such great delight in uttering it.

"Yeah, Eddie, it's been a business," one of us would reply, still chuckling.

"See you next week!"

"We'll be here."

Eddie's appetite for mystery lots was voracious. The number he bought puzzled us, considering what we knew of his finances.

"What do you do with all those mystery lots?" I finally asked one day.

"Take 'em home and go through 'em. Take out everything that strikes my fancy. When I've pulled out what I want, I take the rest over to my table at the flea market. Break 'em down bit by bit. Put a little bit at a time out, five or ten bucks' worth. People figure I'm cleaning out the attic, that I don't know what I've got. So, they're willing to take a shot for five or ten bucks. Think they might be getting something valuable from dumb old Eddie." He flashed his big, impish, Eddie grin. "If I'm lucky, I make a few bucks, then come back over here and get another load."

Eddie never told us whether he had an organized collection. It would have been difficult to build one from mystery lots. We assumed he accumulated whatever came his way, whatever caught his eye.

Grot was Eddie's adjective for mystery lots. That and *drek*.

"Got any good grot lots this week?" he'd ask as he strolled in the front door.

"What is grot?" I once asked.

"I dunno. It's like drek, whatever that is," he replied. Soon, even Tom and I were referring to mystery lots as grot lots.

As time passed, we learned bits and pieces about the flea market trade.

"How much?" Eddie asked one day.

"Fifty bucks."

"Ouch!"

"C'mon Eddie, it can't be that bad. You're going to make a killing on it, and you know it."

"Not likely," he said, rummaging madly through the carton. "I can't mark my stuff up to the moon. I'm an honest businessman, not like old Jack the Ripper . . . the guy who's got the stall next to me at the flea market."

"Eddie, I think you're a bit of a rascal yourself," I said, trying to josh him.

He grinned sheepishly, as if caught with his hand in the cookie jar, then snorted in protest, "You don't know the meaning of the word. Jack the Ripper—that's what everybody calls him—now there's a real rascal! Talk about a con man, he's got more schemes than Planters' got peanuts. I don't know how he gets away with them.

"He gets sheets of uncut dollar bills from the mint. Then cuts 'em so they've got half a bill top and half a bill on the bottom, with the margin running right down the middle. He cuts 'em real neat, so they're the exact same size as a regular dollar bill, only they look real screwed up, like they're a valuable error. Then he puts one of those crazy bills in his wallet. Meanwhile, he's got a few junk coins and silver dollars spread out on his table.

"If anyone shows any interest in the coins, he pipes right up. 'Say, you must be an expert on coins,' he says, kissing up to the mark. 'Maybe you can tell me something about this crazy dollar bill,' he says, pulling the miscut bill out of his wallet. 'Got it the other day. It's the damndest thing I ever saw. Have you ever seen anything like it?' he says, playing real dumb, all the time watching the mark for any sign of interest.

" 'You got to play dumb,' Jack says, 'and let the mark make the first move. He'll look at the bill and assume it's a valuable error. Then he'll get real greedy, try to figure out how to get it away from you real cheap.'

" 'Do you want to sell it?' the mark will ask, and when he does—bingo! All you gotta do is reel him in. You can't be too anxious, though. Gotta play kinda dumb and say something like, 'Gee, I hadn't thought about it, but I suppose I could let it go.' And here, Jack's real proud of himself. 'I was kind of planning to hang on to it,' he'll say. 'I suppose I could let it go, if it's something you could use for your collection. But I'm sure not gonna part with it for a dollar. I'd have to get at least twenty bucks, maybe more.'

"Then Jackie laughs, 'Man, they drag out that twenty bucks so fast it'd make your head spin. Just like shooting ducks in a barrel. They figure the bill is worth a hundred bucks or a thousand or even more. They think they've scored real big, really ripped you off. But the joke's on them. W.C. Fields was right about a sucker born every minute.'"

"I think it was P.T. Barnum who said that," I remarked.

"Whatever," Eddie continued, "The point is, I'm not a con man like old Jack the Ripper. That's why they call him Jack the Ripper, because he loves to rip people off. They also call him Jumpin' Jack, because he hops around from one scam to the next, like a grasshopper in tall clover.

"The emerald scam is one of his favorites," Eddie said. "The emeralds are real enough, but they're junk. I don't know where he gets 'em. They're rough, uncut. They look like pieces of broken Coke bottle glass, only darker. Tells people that he bought 'em earlier in the day from a guy desperate for money, that he practically stole 'em.

"Then, the clincher. 'Look, man,' Jack says, 'I've got a heavy deal coming down in a couple of hours. Guy brought some old coins by a little while ago. I didn't have enough cash to make the deal on the spot, so I told him to come back in a couple of hours. I gotta get liquid fast. Look, you can have the emeralds for what I got in 'em—twenty bucks. It's a steal. I wouldn't even offer 'em to you except I need cash for this other deal.' And they usually bite. Trouble is, the emeralds are only worth about three bucks. You'd be surprised how many people take a shot for twenty bucks.

"Jack's never short of schemes for making a fast buck," Eddie said. "He sells foreign coins three for a quarter. What makes 'em special is that they're the exact same size as a U.S. quarter. He's got a boxful on his table with a sign: *Parking meter change. Three for a quarter*. For twenty-five cents, you get three coins that work just like quarters. It's like getting a sixty-six percent discount.

"I once asked him where he got all the coins. 'That's the sweet part of the deal,' Jack snickered. 'The city separates all the slugs out of the money from parking meters. When they get a bagful, they sell it to me. They're probably real proud of themselves, thinking they're making a few extra bucks on all those junk foreign coins. If they only knew where those coins were going. The coins cost me less than a penny apiece, and I never run out. It seems like whenever I get low, along comes the city with another bag. Hey, I'm just doing my part for recycling and helping working folks save a few bucks along the way,' Jack says.

"If there's one thing old Jack loves more than making a quick buck, it's bragging about it," Eddie said. "No way am I a con artist like old Jack the Ripper."

I never thought Eddie was a con man. I don't think he misrepresented his stamps. He just took advantage of the flea market shopper's instinct for a bargain-priced potential treasure.

The part of the picture Eddie never knew about was the folks who wandered into the office every so often with small albums or dusty old boxes of stamps. "Got these at the flea market," they'd say, "Just wanted to find out if they're worth anything."

The answer was usually the same: "Just beginner material, worth about five or ten dollars. It's not something we're interested in buying, but thanks anyway for coming in." They'd leave with disappointed faces. Occasionally, an album or box would look familiar, and we'd know it had come from Eddie.

Like I said, I never judged Eddie to be a rascal, just a character. Spring, summer, fall, winter, Eddie showed up to negotiate his deals, claim his grot lots, and share his jokes. "Well, it's been a business," he'd say, then, hefting his purchase, "Gotta run, can't keep the chauffeur waiting." We'd all laugh. It was great fun.

I can't remember exactly when Eddie stopped coming in. As mysteriously as he had appeared, he disappeared. Tom and I thought he might have been ill or, perhaps, had an accident, but we had no way of finding out. We never saw Eddie again.

He'll always be one of my favorite characters. I often wonder what happened to him. I hope he's okay, but if not, I know he's set up shop somewhere in that big flea market in the sky.

DO YOU BUY STOLEN STAMPS?

"Do you buy stolen stamps?" asked the larger of two rough-looking men, as he plopped a ragged cardboard carton on Debbie's desk. Debbie, my secretary, was a quiet soul used to greeting pleasant, well-mannered clients. The two scruffy visitors were definitely out of place. They were day laborers by the look of them—dungarees that needed washing, T-shirts that had long since given up being white, cigarette packs bulging under rolled-over sleeves, and enough black earth under their fingernails to plant Iowa corn. They grinned broadly, as if selling stolen stamps were routine business, or, at least, nothing to be ashamed of. Debbie wasn't reassured by their smiles.

Debbie's desk was located at the rear of the reception area of my office in Denver. It was visible from my office. I could see the two rough-looking heavies standing in front of it, and I had heard the remark about stolen stamps. Impulsively, I rushed out to find out what it was all about. If I had stopped to think, I would have called the police first, but I didn't. I just rushed out.

"Can I help you?" I asked, not sure how to handle the situation.

"Yeah, man, we got these stamps for sale," the larger man said, flashing a smile that appeared all the more bright against his dark, unwashed complexion. He gestured to the box as he spoke. The carton was dilapidated and filthy. It was painfully obvious that our visitors weren't stamp collectors.

"Did I hear you say these stamps were stolen?" I asked.

The large man chuckled heartily, his unbridled mirth escaping through a broad, nicotine-stained grin. His partner shared his amusement. Although their behavior wasn't overtly threatening, the initial comment about stolen stamps, their unsavory appearance, and their peculiar amusement, as if they shared an ominous inside joke, made them seem vaguely sinister. A chill went down my spine. Stolen stamps are not a laughing matter.

The larger man watched me, watched my reaction. I felt like a rabbit cornered by wolves. Disturbing possibilities raced through my mind. Then, he said, "Hey, I wuz just kiddin'." And they both burst out laughing, amused by our discomfort. Debbie looked somewhat relieved, but still worried. "Mr. Donaghue over at the hospital sent us," the man continued, offering me a business card. "You're s'posed to call him and tell him what these stamps are worth."

The card was smudged with grimy fingerprints. According to the title beneath the name, Mr. Donaghue was an executive at National Jewish Hospital, an institution well known for its asthma work, especially with children.

"We found the box while we wuz cleaning out his garage, and he told us to bring it on over."

I wasn't the least bit amused. "Wait over there," I said icily, motioning to the waiting area. I took the dilapidated box, which felt like it would fall apart any moment, into my office for a look. The entire contents were covered with fine grit, the kind that you can feel more than see, the kind that leaves you with an urge to wash your hands, that offends your basic notion of how stamps should be cared for. Grit had penetrated everywhere. The collection obviously had lain forgotten for many years. It was a beginner's collection: a small worldwide album, a couple of pounds of mixture on paper, a few approval selections of nominal value, tongs, and a magnifying glass. It had been someone's childhood treasure, but it was in sorry shape now.

I got Mr. Donaghue on the phone. He confirmed that he had sent the box over with instructions to get an offer.

"It's a beginner's collection," I said, preparing to tell him I couldn't use it. "It hasn't much value."

"That's right, I started it as a kid. Had a lot of fun with it, but never followed through. I thought it might have some value after all these years."

"Unfortunately, it doesn't. It's nothing but common stamps, the kind that don't appreciate over time."

"Well, how much could you give me for it?"

"It's really not the kind of thing I'm in the market for."

"How about a hundred bucks?" he asked quickly.

"Frankly, I'd be lucky to get twenty-five dollars retail for it." I bit my tongue as soon as the words were out of my mouth because it wasn't worth even $25.

"Well, just give me a check for whatever is fair. Make it out to the hospital. I'm donating it. You know the good work we do with kids."

The collection was junk, but when he mentioned donation and the work with kids, I knew I was trapped. I would to have to buy it.

"Okay," I agreed, "I can give you twenty-five dollars for it, but that's stretching it." It was the truth. Nevertheless, I suddenly found myself feeling guilty that I hadn't offered more.

"Fine," he said, "and thanks. I sure appreciate it."

At least, the money would go to a good cause.

I took a check from my desk drawer and returned to Debbie's desk. The two jokers were still seated in the waiting area. They looked up as I instructed Debbie in a clearly audible, businesslike voice, "Call the bank and ask them to transfer a quarter of a million dollars into our account from our line of credit to make this check good."

Astonishment struck them like lightning. The larger man slapped his leg and, turning to his buddy, exclaimed, "God damn! I told you we should've ripped it off!"

They jumped up and rushed over to Debbie's desk. The larger man spoke again, "We found that box in Donaghue's garage. On the way over here, it set right between us on the seat. Man, we coulda just taken it home with us. I told Leroy we shoulda kept it. Quarter of a million bucks!" He turned to his bewildered partner and, shaking his head, repeated rhetorically, "Damn, I told ya we shoulda ripped it off!"

His candor surprised me. Without the slightest embarrassment, he openly admitted that he and his friend had contemplated stealing the box of stamps, but had chosen not to. Now, learning that the collection was worth a fortune, he expressed profound and animated remorse for not having done so. How remarkable, I thought. How often does someone admit openly and unabashedly that he feels like a fool for being honest?

My remark puzzled Debbie. She hadn't yet reached for the phone. She knew I was up to something. Meanwhile, I began writing the check. "Lucky you brought that collection in," I said as I wrote. "It looked like junk, but it contained a copy of the Southeast Zambezi, bluish-purple, 12 drachma on inverted laid paper." I looked up at them to emphasize my point. "That stamp is so rare that no one even knows it exists."

The two jokers stood silently, solemnly at the desk, unaware that my words were just mumbo-jumbo. They exchanged confused, uncomfortable glances, struggling inwardly with regret that they had let the opportunity of a lifetime slip between their fingers.

When I had finished writing, I handed the check to the larger man. He looked at it, frowned a bewildered frown, then, as the joke dawned on him, laughed.

"Twenty-five bucks! Look at this Leroy—twenty-five bucks!" he said, showing the check to his befuddled companion. "Hey, you got us good, mister. Quarter of a million . . . you really had me goin'!" His broad, beaming smile returned.

"Stolen stamps," I said, smiling back.

"Yeah, I had you goin', didn't I? The look on this little gal's face was too much," he said, savoring the thought. "But you got us right back with that quarter-million—and real good, too! You're okay, man," he said, thrusting the dubious compliment on me.

They turned to leave, and as they reached the front door, I couldn't resist a parting gibe, "Hey, don't lose that quarter of a million on the way to the hospital."

"No way, man," the larger man replied, still grinning. He tucked the check into his shirt pocket and patted it ceremoniously. "This bread's safe with us, don't you worry none." The door slammed shut behind them. Debbie and I looked at each other, and laughed and laughed and laughed.

EASY COME, EASY GO

There are those dealers who regard buying stamps from the public as a purely mathematical exercise at best and a barely tolerable nuisance at worst. I, however, am one of those dealers who enjoys buying from the public. One pleasure of buying from the public is meeting a lot of different people, and behind each one lies a story. A few of those stories remain with you a long, long time. The Winters' tale is one of them.

Mrs. Winters was in her seventies when I first met her during the spring of 1982. She had invited me to her home to make an offer on her late husband's stamp collection. She lived in an older home nestled in a tangle of shrubs and trees just beginning to show signs of April greening.

Decades before, when the house was new and the Winters first moved in, it had been located out in the country, in the highlands west of Denver. Now, it was surrounded by housing developments, themselves approaching middle age. Only its greenery buffered it from restless urban sprawl. Later in the season, tightly knit undergrowth would completely hide the house from neighbors and passers-by alike.

To some, the Winters home appeared unkempt. To me, it had the simple unpretentiousness of a pair of old shoes whose comfort outweighs their appearance.

Denver's dry, technically semiarid, climate is a blessing for philatelists. It keeps stamps fresh, bright, and looking new for years. That's why the Winters collection was so wonderfully well preserved. Begun before the Depression, it was loaded with better mint U.S. stamps and plate blocks, including Zeppelin plate blocks. It was the kind of collection stamp dealers relish finding.

"The collection is gorgeous," I said to Mrs. Winters, who was seated across from me at the dining room table. Big, green Scott albums lay spread out across the table.

"Thank you," she said. "Harry was a very serious collector. 'Settle for nothing less than the best!' he always liked to say. I enjoyed the stamps, too . . . they kind of grew on me," she mused. "Harry and I shared a lot of interests. I guess that's why we got along so well together."

"Your husband did a first-rate job," I said. "They just don't come any nicer." And it was true. Most collections are strictly routine: the same old stamps in predictably mediocre condition, thinning out rapidly at the point catalogue values begin to rise. The Winters collection was the exception. Premium quality copies filled almost every page.

I took my time paging through it, not because it was difficult to evaluate, but because it isn't often you get the opportunity to savor such pristine gems.

While I enjoyed the collection and busied myself making notes, Mrs. Winters served refreshments in China cups—tea for me, black coffee for her. We chatted.

"You both collected?" I asked.

"Harry did the collecting. I just watched. He explained things as he went along, and I enjoyed the stamps—they're so colorful, the engraving's so beautiful—but didn't get involved in buying or mounting them. I just enjoyed them, and enjoyed Harry enjoying them. We enjoyed a lot of things together."

"Well, he built a remarkable collection."

"Harry was a remarkable man," she said, taking a sip of coffee. "I think I knew that the first time I met him." She paused, and, peering over the top of the cup, said, "I married the boss, you know." She smiled slyly, an immensely proud little smile, as if she had done something exceedingly clever. And I knew a story was coming.

"It was back in the Depression. I didn't have a nickel to my name. I needed work, and, believe me, back then work was tough to get. Harry owned a market. It was on the outskirts of town in those days. Nothing fancy, sawdust on the floor, bales of hay out front, a good, old-fashioned neighborhood store. Being on the outskirts of town, the store served a lot of farm customers, carried seed and feed, tack, and anything else you could make an honest buck on."

Mrs. Winters looked ten or fifteen years younger than she actually was. She wore her years well, appeared remarkably fit. She impressed me as a tough yet kind woman who regarded obstacles as challenges, a woman made all the stronger by struggle, a woman kept fit by hard work. Her voice was energetic, and her crystal-blue eyes sparkled as she spoke.

"I'd been to see about a job in a leather goods plant. They made saddles, bridles, that kind of stuff. It was down the road from Harry's store. I didn't get the job and was walking back toward town—didn't want to spend the money for a trolley ride—when I stopped at Harry's. I hoped to get a drink of water there.

" 'Haven't seen you around here before,' Harry said when I walked in. He knew everybody in the neighborhood.

" 'Just been up at Hornsby's Saddlery about the bookkeeper's job,' I told him.

" 'I can see why you didn't get the job,' he chuckled. I was puzzled, annoyed, embarrassed, and insulted. I thought maybe he meant that I looked too young for the job. I was young, but I didn't think I was *that* young. Anyway, my face turned beet red. I'd been looking for a job for weeks. I'd been all over the city. I was tired and depressed, in no mood to be insulted. I turned to walk out, but he called after me.

" 'Hey, I didn't mean anything by it.'

"I stopped and turned to face him. 'You must have talked to Mrs. Hornsby about the job.'

"I nodded. Harry's smile was a mile wide, and his big white teeth were as straight as piano keys.

" 'That was your problem,' he said. 'Mrs. Hornsby isn't about to hire someone as young and pretty as you are. Not around old Bill Hornsby—that's her husband. They don't call him Wild Bill for nothing. Please don't take offense. I didn't mean anything by it. How about that glass of water?'

"I'd worried that I was too young or too skinny. At the time, I *was* pretty skinny. I hadn't been getting too much to eat—couldn't afford it. But if I could believe what Harry told me, I hadn't gotten the job because I was too attractive. I was kind of flattered by his remark.

"Harry got the me the glass of water. We chatted. Looking back, I know I was charmed that first moment he smiled at me. He was a big man, cheerful and good-natured. When he smiled, it was like walking out into a bright, warm July morning. I liked that about him.

" 'So, you're a bookkeeper?' he said as I stood there, glass of water in hand.

" 'Yes, and a pretty good one, too,' I replied, perhaps immodestly, but at that moment, I was in no mood to be modest. I was disappointed at not getting the job. I wasn't looking forward to the walk back downtown.

" 'You're not from around here, are you? I mean, not from Denver?'

" 'No, how did you know?'

" 'Your accent, girl. Upper Midwest . . . Minnesota, I'd guess.'

" 'You're right,' I said, draining the tumbler. 'Thanks for the water. I've got to get going. It's a long walk back downtown.'

" 'Say, don't be in such a hurry,' he said. "I've been thinking I might be able to use a bookkeeper. Lots of good folks are buying on credit these days. They come in, take this or that, and say, "Just put it on my tab, Harry." Trouble is, sometimes when I'm real busy, I forget to make a note of it. I don't know how much it's costing me.'

"He smiled at me. I listened, wondering if I were hearing him right, wondering if he were offering me a job. 'Course there's plenty of other work to be done, too,' he said. 'It wouldn't be one of those la-de-da jobs for someone who's afraid to get her hands dirty. I could pay six dollars a week—that includes all day Saturday. You'd get Sundays off. What do say?'

"I liked Harry Winters. I liked his great big happy face and his wide-as-the-sky sunshine smile. *And* I was pretty desperate. I was living on borrowed money, scraping by from day to day. The Depression was terrible. I just had to get a job, so I said, 'Yes.'

" 'Great!' Harry exclaimed. 'That's wonderful. I'm going to have a real organization now. Say, I don't even know your name!'

" 'Katrina Lindstrom. And I don't know yours!'

" 'Harry Winters, Miss Lindstrom. Just like the sign out front says—WINTERS MERCANTILE CO. HARRY WINTERS, PROPRIETOR.'

"And that's how I met the boss," Kate Winters said. She rose. From an end table she fetched a photo mounted in an ornate gold frame. "Here's a picture of Harry and me back in 1932. I was twenty-two then. Can it have been fifty years ago? It seems like only yesterday," she said sighing, handing me the photo.

I looked at it. Mrs. Winters was modest. She had, indeed, been a beauty. Her hair had been blond then. It still was, but much of the sunny yellow had faded with time, just as the harsh tones of the black-and-white depression-era photo had faded, mellowing over the years into a soft, caramel-colored sepia. A youthful Kate and Harry posed on the wooden planking in front of a white storefront. The sign above their heads read WINTERS MERCANTILE CO. Harry's arm wrapped around her shoulder, and hers was around his waist. Harry appeared somewhat older than Kate, perhaps in his mid-thirties. They wore smiles. They were young and happy. They didn't have a care in the world.

"I kept the books, such as they were," Kate Winters continued. "Mostly just IOUs and such. Harry could be a little sloppy when it came to keeping track of how much people owed. Times were really tough. A lot of people were out of work and destitute. Harry carried a lot folks . . . longer than I would have. I told him he should give some serious thought to tightening up his credit policy, that he could be making a lot more money. Harry's credit policy was simple," she laughed, putting her hand to her mouth, suddenly seized by the humor of it. "If you didn't have money, you got credit. Some people hadn't paid their bills in months. But Harry was very forgiving. Even though I'd never admit it to him, I liked that about Harry. He was such a helluva nice guy—pardon my French.

"I worked real hard. Got to know the customers, learned who really was hard up and who was just taking advantage of Harry's good nature—and quite a few were. Tightened up the receivables, organized the store, made room for new products. Convinced Harry that he ought to keep an eye to the future, that he ought to sell radios, appliances, and the like. There was a lot of work to do, stocking shelves, waiting on customers, making deliveries, doing books. Even though it was the Depression, the store hummed.

"My first Saturday on the job, Mr. Hornsby and his wife came in. Harry and I were behind the counter near the door. 'Hi, Harry,' Hornsby said. 'Say, who's the new clerk?'

" 'Kate Lindstrom,' Harry replied. 'Hard worker and ace bookkeeper.'

" 'How'd I miss out on a prize like you?' Hornsby said, his roving eye wandering unconsciously up, down, and over me. 'I've been trying to find a good bookkeeper.'

"Mrs. Hornsby took his arm and harrumphed. 'Let's not waste all day,' she said. 'These folks have more important things to do than listen to you twaddle on.'

"As they were leaving, Mr. Hornsby leaned over and said to me, 'If Harry don't treat you right, come on over to the saddlery and see me personally. There'll be a job waiting for you.' Mrs. Hornsby harrumphed again. Neither she nor I let on that we'd met. The moment they were out the door, Harry and I looked at each other and burst out laughing.

"I was a hard worker," Kate Winters said. "It just came naturally. And I liked Harry Winters. He was a good man and a good boss— honest, generous, and considerate. That's why people traded with him. They liked him. It was the secret of his success.

"After I'd worked there for several months, I decided to ask for a raise. I thought I deserved it. On the other hand, jobs were scarce as hen's teeth then. One didn't go about making a pest of themselves and risk losing a good thing. A little voice inside me said, *Keep your mouth shut and be thankful that you've got work.* Another little voice said, *Be brave! Go ahead, ask for a raise.* I debated for days. Finally, I decided to give it a try. Harry was so nice, I didn't think he would refuse me.

"It was Saturday evening. I waited until we'd locked up, counted the receipts, and put them in the safe. 'Mr. Winters, sir,' I said, in my most formal, respectful voice, 'Would you think it out of line if I asked for a raise? You know how hard I work.'

"Harry didn't answer right away. He suddenly looked very serious and thoughtful—even distressed—as if he were going to have to say something unpleasant, something he would have preferred not to say. And that made me very nervous.

" 'Well, you've been here about six months,' he said at last, 'and I knew that sooner or later you'd bring up the subject of a raise, so I've been giving the matter some thought myself. You're a good worker,' he said, counting off the points one finger at a time. 'You're punctual, you have initiative, you don't need close supervision, the customers like you, you're trustworthy, you've got a great head for business . . . and you're very beautiful.'

"Again, I blushed beet red. When I'm embarrassed or flattered, I can't help it," Kate Winters said to me.

" 'But I don't think a raise is in the cards,' Harry continued.

"I knew beforehand that it was likely that I wouldn't get the raise, nevertheless, I was disappointed. I couldn't complain, since six dollars a week was more than a lot of folks made. A lot more didn't have jobs at all. Perhaps I'd been too greedy.

"Harry untied his apron and removed it as he spoke. Placing it on the counter, he took my hand in his and said, 'Kate, no question about it, you're worth every cent I pay you and more. I won't argue with you about a raise, but I'd really rather have you as a partner. Would you be my partner?'

"I couldn't believe my ears. Almost afraid to ask, I said, 'Are you asking me to marry you?'

"He nodded. 'Yes, Kate. I'm asking you to marry me.'

"I was surprised, thrilled, overwhelmed. I'd liked Harry from the first day we met and knew I'd never find a more wonderful man.

" 'Harry,' I said, 'you've got yourself a partner!'

" 'Hallelujah!' he shouted, grabbing my waist, lifting me right off the floor. 'C'mon, we're gonna buy the best steak dinner and the biggest bottle of champagne in Denver, and then we're gonna dance until Monday morning!'"

"The store grew and prospered right through the thirties and the war years," Kate Winters said. "After the war, we sold appliances like they were going out of style. In the 1950s, we added TVs. Business boomed. We made a darn good living. I was lucky, a girl who came to town in the middle of the Depression with nothing but the clothes on her back and no prospects—damn lucky to find such a terrific husband. It was a dream come true. The only thing missing was children. We wanted a family. We tried to have one, but something just wasn't right. The doctors didn't know what. They ran tests. They said they couldn't find any medical reason why we shouldn't be able to have kids. They were as puzzled as we were.

"Then little Reggie came along. One day without warning, mysteriously, and at long last, I was pregnant. We'd resigned ourselves to not having children, so it seemed like a miracle. Harry literally jumped for joy when I told him the news.

"Little Reggie was our only child, the center of our lives," she said, sipping her coffee, "and I'm afraid we spoiled him terribly. We bought this place—it was out in the country back then—so Reggie could have a pony. I can still see Harry leading that pinto pony around the back lot with little Reggie in the saddle. 'Giddyup! Giddyup!' Reggie would shout, his little legs not halfway down to the stirrups, urging the pony on. Harry took him everywhere—the zoo, museums, movies—and bought him everything he wanted. No child ever had more love lavished on him. Reggie was our treasure, the child that was never supposed to happen, a gift from God. Whatever he wanted, he got. Harry just couldn't say no to him. Reggie was such a darling.

"Let me show you some pictures," she said, retrieving a photo album from one of the bedrooms. She laid it on the table in front of me and opened it carefully. There I met Reggie, forever frozen in fading Kodacolor: Reggie in his cowboy outfit, six-gun ready to fire; Reggie on his brand-new bike, tilting precariously to one side on trainer wheels; Reggie cocking his arm to pass a football slightly too large for his ten-year-old hand; Reggie at the zoo, mouth open in a shout, a balloon in one hand, the other pointing at elephants. Page after page, Reggie laughed, jumped, and shouted. He was a deliriously happy youngster.

"Reggie was a good boy," Kate Winters said wistfully, pensively, leaving me unsure whether the sentiment was a happy or a sad one. "The joy of our lives.

"Harry wanted him to go to college. And he did for a year. Harry bought him a brand-new, bright-red Mustang convertible. Reggie loved it. Then Harry had a heart attack. He died while Reggie was away at school that first year. I kept the store going for a few months after he died, but my heart wasn't in it. It just wasn't the same without Harry. Besides, we'd saved our money, and I really didn't need to work, so I sold the store.

"Reggie never made it through his second year at college. Said it was a waste of time, that Harry and I had done perfectly well without college, so he didn't see why he needed it. I don't think he studied as much as he should have. His grades weren't that good. Whenever he called home, it was for money. While he was alive, Harry gave him whatever he asked for. I did too, for that matter. We loved Reggie so much.

"He wrecked the Mustang, then wanted a new Corvette. He pleaded and pleaded for it, so I finally bought it for him. After he quit college, he held a variety of jobs, but they never seemed to last long.

"Reggie was spirited and headstrong. He liked expensive clothes and new cars. I figured it was just the impetuousness of youth, that he'd grow out of it. Finally, I told him it was time to get serious about making a living, so he decided to open a restaurant.

"It was going to be the best restaurant in Denver," Kate Winters said. "First-class all the way. When Reggie was enthusiastic about something, he gave it his all. No halfway measures. Only the best would do. He spent a small fortune decorating it. I know. I lent him the money. He hired the best chefs, made the waiters wear formal dress, aimed for an affluent clientele.

"In my opinion, it was a little flashy, too glitzy. But, it reflected Reggie's personality. A restaurant critic wrote it up. He said something to the effect that 'the ambiance is assertively avant-garde rather than discreetly elegant. The menu is bold and daring rather than safely traditional.' Reggie just loved the review, thought it was the best thing ever.

"And it is quite the place. But for some reason, it's never taken off. Maybe Denver just isn't ready for that kind of restaurant. Still, I have great hopes . . . for Reggie's sake.

"Every couple of months, I have to help him out with cash. He always says, 'Don't worry, Mom, it's about to take off . . . just takes time to get established . . . any day now.' So, I've kept the restaurant going for three years now. I try to think positively, but sometimes I have my doubts. I just hope for his sake that it works out," Kate Winters said with a sigh.

"Reggie buys a lot of new clothes. I've thought perhaps he's a little extravagant, but he always says, 'You've got to look successful to be successful!'

"I want to think the restaurant will succeed. I pray that it will, but sometimes I just don't know. I don't think Reggie gives much thought to how much it costs. Maybe he thinks I'm so well off that I can afford anything. Unfortunately, the well isn't bottomless. I've just wanted to spare him the terrible poverty of my childhood."

Kate Winters paused, no longer smiling. The warm sunshine, the fond memories of her wonderful early days, had faded. It was evident that Reggie was slowly sucking her dry, frittering away the savings it had taken a lifetime to accumulate. I wondered if he knew—or cared. Clearly, Reggie's exploits were taking their toll on Kate Winters, but she was too strong to break down.

"All that's left now is the house and the land—a couple of acres— and the stamp collection. I get Social Security, which is enough. My needs are minimal. Reggie needs twenty thousand dollars. That's why I have to sell the collection."

Kate Winters forced a smile. She wasn't about to allow sadness to overwhelm her. She was a product of the Depression, tested by the severest of times. She was strong, durable, hard working, resourceful, shrewd, determined, and uncomplaining. She had been a wonderful wife and a devoted mother. She was absolutely selfless. How ironic, I thought, that she ended up with a son like Reggie.

"The collection is worth about thirty-five thousand dollars," I said. "I can write you a check for that amount right now." I was eager to buy it. Harry had lavished the same care and attention on the collection that he had lavished on Reggie. It lacked for nothing.

"How much is the airmail album worth?" she asked. "I'd kind of like to keep it, if that won't reduce the offer by too much."

"The airmails are worth about thirteen thousand."

"I'll just keep them for the time being," she said, pulling the album across the table toward her until it rested beside the photo album of Reggie's snapshots.

The airmail album was gorgeous, the best single volume of the collection. I hated to see it slip between my fingers. I wished she would sell it, but at the same time I was happy that she could keep at least part of Harry's collection.

I wrote a check for $22,000, wondering if Reggie was aware that his mother was scraping the bottom of the barrel. Then it occurred to me that she didn't want him to know. I remembered her remark about wanting to spare him the "terrible poverty of my childhood." I couldn't help thinking that Reggie ought to be more concerned about his mother and less about his extravagant lifestyle.

"Thanks very much," I said, handing her the check. "You've got my number in case you decide to sell the airmails."

Kate Winters smiled as I left. She was cheerful, I decided, because it pleased her to make her son happy. They don't make 'em like her any more, I thought as I pulled out of her driveway.

A few weeks later, Kate Winters called back. Was I still interested in the airmails, and if so, could I come out that afternoon?

"Thanks very much for coming on such short notice," she said, greeting me at the front door. "I guess I'm going to have to sell the airmails, after all. I should have called earlier, but I kept putting it off."

"No problem, glad I can help," I said, knowing immediately that the money was for Reggie, marveling at how quickly he had gone through the $22,000.

"Reggie's getting married," she said, beaming, "and he's going to get a new van and boat. He's got them all picked out." She was genuinely happy for him.

Again, I wondered: Did Reggie know that his extravagancies were taking his mother's last $13,000? Did he care? Would her home and acreage be the next—and last remaining—assets sold to support Reggie's lifestyle? I hoped not. I hoped with all my heart that Kate Winters would keep her home and land. Then a terrible thought: *Kind, selfless, devoted Kate Winters probably would sell her house and land to raise money for Reggie.* That's the kind of woman she was. And after the home and land were gone, then what? I didn't want to know. The thought was simply too depressing.

What kind of a man was this Reggie? I tried to visualize him, to visualize his lifestyle, but came up with only unpleasant, disagreeable images.

The green Scott airmail album rested center table. I looked it over quickly. It was just as I had last seen it. The Zeppelin plate blocks were still safely tucked in their mounts. I took a check from my attaché case and began writing. Kate waited patiently, happily across the table from me. When I finished, I handed her the check.

"Thank you very much," she said, smiling. She looked as happy as any human being I had ever seen. Strong, hardworking, selfless, heart-of-gold Katrina Winters. You're one helluva woman, I thought. And, in that long, uncomfortable moment before I would say goodbye to Kate Winters for the last time, my eyes were again drawn to the mantel, to the time-faded photograph taken half a century before. The smiling faces of a young Kate and Harry, arms around one another, in front of the Winters Mercantile Co., ready to take on the world, looked down on us. Suddenly, I was profoundly glad that I had never met—and would never meet—Reggie Winters.

HIGH PLAINS DRIFTER

The Drifter got his name one late-summer afternoon while Debbie and I watched from our sixth-floor office window in the Century Bank Building, as he walked to his car parked at the end of the block. He owned a white Cadillac Eldorado convertible with a red leather interior. He'd parked it with the top down.

It was easy to imagine spurs jingling on his boots, as I watched him saunter down the block. Thin and haunting as the desert wind, the theme song from the movie *High Plains Drifter*, wandered into my head. Unconsciously, I started to whistle it softly.

Debbie said, "High Plains Drifter," perhaps referring to the theme song or perhaps, to the man six floors below.

"Yes," I replied, "the High Plains Drifter."

And the name stuck.

The Drifter was a tall, thin man in his early forties, dressed in a snap-pocket western shirt, sports jacket, and cowboy boots. He vaguely resembled Clint Eastwood. He was a quiet man, who liked to play his cards close to the vest. Whenever we sat down to do business, I did most of the talking.

I first met the Drifter in the summer of 1980. The oil boom was on and Denver was awash in petrodollars. Wildcatters, wheeler-dealers, and speculators from all over had converged on the city. They drove fancy cars, made big deals, and carried fat rolls of hundred-dollar bills. The Drifter was an oil landsman from Oklahoma scouting properties in eastern Colorado—out on the high plains. He traveled a lot, bouncing back and forth between Tulsa, Houston, Dallas, and Denver. We never learned much more about him.

The Drifter dropped in on an irregular basis—sometimes weeks apart—with stamps for sale. According to him, he'd inherited a stamp collection from an uncle and was disposing of it bit by bit.

He'd walk in, plop some stamps on my desk, and ask, "What'll you give me for these?"

I'd look them over and make an offer. If he liked it, he'd say "Okay." If not, he'd say, "Thanks anyway. Maybe next time," and be on his way.

One afternoon he dropped by with a complete mint set of Nebraska overprint sheets. Sheet sets of Nebraska overprints are very rare and, in those days, catalogued more than $25,000.

"My uncle got these from a postmaster he knew in Nebraska," the Drifter said, laying the manila envelope that held the sheets on my desk.

"He told me they'd be worth a fortune someday. You see, he had an in with a postmaster. Got him to do something against the rules. That's why these sheets are so rare."

The Drifter paused and began to extract the sheets from the envelope.

"There was a rule against precancelling Nebraska overprints, so my uncle figured that if he could get the postmaster to precancel them, he'd have something a thousand times rarer and more valuable than normal."

The Drifter pushed the sheets to my side of the desk and came as close to smiling as I'd ever seen him.

The set was fresh and bright as the day it was printed—and precancelled "Hastings, Nebr." I knew the Drifter was a man who appreciated plain speaking, so I didn't waste words.

"Too bad they're precancelled," I said. "As such, they're worth maybe five hundred to a thousand dollars. And that's just a guess."

"They're a helluva lot rarer than unprecancelled sheets," the Drifter objected. "They ought to be worth five times or ten times what a regular set's worth!"

"If supply were the key, you'd be right. Unfortunately, demand is the key. Despite their rarity, there's virtually no demand for precancelled sets. You can't get premium prices for something that's tough to sell. In fact, just the opposite. You've got to discount it to make it go away.

"If your uncle had just left them alone," I added, "they'd be worth ten or twenty times what they're worth precancelled."

The Drifter scowled slightly, not pleased by the news that his uncle's cleverness had backfired.

"So, what's your best offer?"

I had no idea what I'd do with 100 complete sets of Nebraska overprints precancelled "Hastings, Nebr." I thought for a long moment, then decided that at five dollars a set I couldn't go wrong.

"Five hundred bucks," I said.

"I thought I heard you say up to a thousand dollars a minute ago?" the Drifter shot back.

"I did, but it's a risky buy. At five hundred, I'm willing to gamble, at a thousand, I'm not. It won't hurt my feelings if you pass. You might get more elsewhere, and you're welcome to try. I'm just telling you what they're worth to me here and now."

The stone-faced Drifter eyed me for a long moment. For my part, I didn't care if I bought the sheets or not.

"Okay," he said. "But I've got a feeling you're getting the best of this old country boy."

"How would you like the check made out?" I asked, pulling a check from the drawer.

"Cash," he replied.

I was about to tell him that he could verify my check with the bank downstairs when he added: "Greenbacks . . . you know, folding money."

Then I realized it wasn't a question of whether my check was good or not. He was one of those folks who just liked cash.

"Okay," I said, and we went downstairs to the bank. I cashed a check and counted out the bills for him.

"Thanks," he said, folding the money and stuffing it in his front pants pocket.

"You got any other stamps?" I asked.

"Well, I don't know all that much about stamps, but my uncle had a nice looking album full of Columbians."

My first thought was that the uncle had made a specialized collection of varieties of the two-cent Columbian commemoratives.

"Mint or used? Any high values?" I asked.

"Got the whole shootin' match: mint, used, complete sets, blocks, part sheets, you name it—an album full.

Excitement welled up as I visualized the collection: mint and used singles, mint and used blocks, inscription strips, covers, cancels, and who knows what else. Every dealer knows that extraordinary sleeper collections exist, but never really expects them to walk through his door. The news had my blood racing. I wanted to see the collection.

"When could you bring in the album?"

"Maybe next time I'm in town." His expression remained as vague as his comment.

"When would that be?" I pressed.

"Hard to say," he replied. Then, "Oh well, gotta be on my way."

During the next couple of weeks, I anxiously waited for the Drifter to show up again. I thought about the Columbians every day. A comprehensive, carefully formed specialized collection could easily be worth $100,000, $200,000, or more! An uncle with enough savvy to precancel a whole set of Nebraska overprint sheets with the idea that they'd be worth a fortune one day—even though he had guessed wrong—just might have put together the Columbian collection of the century.

Finally, the Drifter showed up.

"Brought you those Columbians I mentioned," he said, setting a slim gray album on my desk.

I pulled it toward me reverently. The moment I'd dreamed of for the past couple of weeks was at hand. I opened it and flipped through the pages, back to front. The Drifter had been true to his word, it was loaded with Columbians: complete sets, mint and used, blocks and part sheets. It was a delightful specialized collection.

Unfortunately, the collection contained stamps of Colombia, not U.S. Columbian commemoratives.

I didn't know whether to laugh or cry.

The Drifter waited for me to speak.

"Nice collection," I said. They were the only words that came to mind.

"I figured you'd like it." Then he asked, "What's your offer?"

"Look, maybe you ought to keep it. It's worth maybe a couple of hundred bucks, that's all."

The Drifter frowned. But I wasn't particularly happy either. First, the precancelled Nebraska overprint stamps, now the Colombian collection. The Drifter's stamps seemed to have a way of disappointing both of us.

"Two hundred dollars?" the Drifter said. "That's all? From the way you talked, I figured it'd be worth big bucks. What's goin' on here, anyway?"

"When I said Columbians were valuable, I thought you had the U.S. Columbian Exposition stamps, not stamps from the country of Colombia."

The Drifter frowned, as if to say, "What's the difference?"

"U.S. Columbian stamps are worth a lot of money. Your uncle's Colombian collection is nice, but the sets are mostly inexpensive. Sorry. Like I said, you're welcome to keep it."

The Drifter mulled over my offer for a long moment, eyeing me with his unsettling stare. Then he spoke, "Okay, I'll take the two hundred—cash."

We repeated our trip to the bank lobby. Now I had a marginal Colombian collection to add to the shelf that contained the still unsold Nebraska overprint precancels.

Third time's a charm, I thought on my way back upstairs. Next time he'll bring in something really worthwhile.

"You said you liked coins," the Drifter said on his next visit. He set a blue velvet display case on my desk.

I don't collect coins, but, occasionally, I keep a coin if it strikes my fancy. I had mentioned that to the Drifter on a previous visit. The blue velvet case contained forty beautiful silver medals nestled in individual recessed spaces. It was the kind of set marketed to collectors by private mints.

I picked up one of the medals by its edge to examine it. The inscription "Sterling Collector's Guild" was neatly hallmarked on the edge. Sterling silver, I thought to myself.

"You know that coin dealers are only paying about melt value for this kind of stuff," I said.

"That's what I've been told," the Drifter allowed.

"Looks like you've got about forty ounces here, more or less. Silver's right at ten dollars an ounce. I could offer four hundred for the set."

The price of silver had fluctuated drastically in 1980, approaching $50 an ounce before the bottom fell out. At the then-current market price of $10 an ounce, it seemed like a bargain.

"Sound's fair to me," the Drifter said.

I slid the blue velvet case into my desk drawer. The Drifter and I took the elevator to the bank lobby, where I paid him $400 in cash.

"Thanks," he said, tucking the money in his pocket.

"My pleasure," I replied.

He smiled, and it pleased me that at least one deal had gone right.

Toward the end of the day, when the hustle and bustle had died down, I pulled case out of the drawer to inspect medals more closely. Their brilliant silver finish contrasted nicely against rich blue velvet. What a beautiful set, I thought, picking up one of the medals. I was careful to hold it by its edges so I wouldn't leave smudges on its brilliant proof-like surface.

Then I noticed something out of place. Part of the medal's edge had chipped—actually, *flaked* is a better word. The area underneath the chip looked brassy. I grabbed a magnifying glass. To my great surprise, the coin had been plated.

How can it be? I thought. The edge is hallmarked as sterling.

I checked the inscription on the edge, then realized I had misinterpreted it. The inscription read "Sterling Collector's Guild." Nowhere did the word *silver* appear. I could have kicked myself. Boy, what a dope! I thought. You just paid $400 for 40 silver plated medals that are worth maybe fifty cents each—if that.

There was nothing I could do. The Drifter was long gone. I didn't know his address or telephone number. I had no way to get in touch with him.

I wonder if he knew? I thought. I wonder if he did it on purpose? I'll find out next time he comes in, I assured myself. He's sure as hell not going to get away with it.

Time passed, but the High Plains Stamp Drifter never came back.

If you see a fellow who vaguely resembles Clint Eastwood driving a white Cadillac Eldorado convertible with a red interior, let me know.

I've got a score to settle with him.

TO HAVE AND TO HAVE NOT

I don't think I'll ever forget the discovery of the second copy of the world's rarest stamp, the British Guiana one-cent magenta.

It was back in the 1970s. I had just walked through the front door of Denver stamp dealer Woodrow B. Goode's shop.

"Steve, wait until you see what I've got!" Woody burst out, waving a black stock card containing a ruby-red piece of paper. He was literally jumping for joy.

"I've found a second copy of the world's rarest stamp!"

Although there are other stamps of which only a single copy is known, the one-cent magenta is certainly the most glamorous. At the time, the only known copy belonged to Irwin Weinberg, who had paid $280,000 for it. Now, Woody claimed to have a second one right there in his hand!

Woody was the most unlikely person—yet paradoxically one of the most likely—to find such a stamp. He traveled extensively, seemed to know everybody, and loved to deal, deal, deal. If ever a soul were at home in the world of philatelic deal making, it was Woody. He glided in and out of stamp deals with the effortless grace of a porpoise scooting across fair-weather seas.

"I've got a call into New York," he said. "I'm going to have the stamp expertized, then auction it off, probably in the next Rarities of the World Sale." He waved the black stock card jubilantly as he spoke.

"I should probably call *Linn's Stamp News* and *Stamp Collector*," he said. "I mean, it's like stop the presses. I've got front page news!"

At that moment, the magnitude of the situation began to sink in. If true, this find would be the biggest philatelic news story of the decade, if not the century. And it was unfolding right before my very eyes. A torrent of thoughts rushed through my head: *A second copy of the world's rarest stamp! Here in Denver! Discovered by Woody B. Goode! Where did he get it? How much would it be worth?*

"What do you think, Steve? Is this incredible or what?" Woody bubbled.

"Maybe you ought to wait until after the stamp is expertized before announcing it to the press," I suggested.

"You're right," he said, nodding affirmatively. "No use jumping the gun. But I know it's going to come back genuine."

Pessimism was not part of Woody's nature.

"Where'd you find it, anyway?"

"In a junk collection. Can you believe it?"

Just then, the phone rang, and Woody rushed to pick it up.

"May I see the stamp while you're on the phone?"

"Sure," he said, tossing me the stock card as if it contained nothing more than a nickel stamp.

"Woody B. Goode Stamps," he said, picking up the phone. Then, "Yes, I called about the one-cent magenta. I've found a second copy!"

I picked up the stock card and looked closely at the rarity. It was magnificent: bright, fresh, and undamaged. Its corners had been trimmed like those of the other known copy, giving it a telltale octagonal shape. It isn't common knowledge that the one-cent magenta wasn't issued with trimmed corners. Other contemporary stamps from British Guiana are rectangular in shape. That both copies should be similarly trimmed seemed unusual. But that wasn't the most interesting fact. The stamp on the stock card had been printed by offset lithography.

Images printed by offset lithography are broken down into a series of dots, the kind that are readily apparent in a newspaper photo. And they were readily apparent on Woody's stamp. Offset lithography didn't come into commercial use until long after the one-cent magenta was printed. The original one-cent magenta was printed by typography. The stamp on the stock card was a reproduction.

Woody was talking animatedly on the phone. I tried to get his attention, but he refused to be distracted.

"I'll send it right away," he said to the unseen caller. "Do you think half a million dollars' insurance is adequate?"

Again, I tried to get Woody's attention. I wanted to spare him the trouble and embarrassment of sending off a reproduction, but he would have none of it. He waved me off, looking mildly annoyed. So I shrugged and let him continue.

Shortly, he hung up and strolled back to the counter, rubbing his hands.

"It's all set," he said. "The stamp's going in for expertizing. I think the best place to sell it would be in Robert Siegel's next Rarities of the World Sale, don't you? Say, what's so important that you have to interrupt me in the middle of a long distance call?"

"Your stamp's a reproduction," I said. "I just thought you would like to have known that while you were on the phone."

"Reproduction? How would you know? You're not an expert," he said haughtily, grabbing the stock card. He had discovered the world's second one-cent magenta. How dare I question it?

"You don't have to be an expert to see the dot structure in the printing," I said.

"So?"

"The dot structure is used in offset lithography. It's a photomechanical process. It wasn't in general commercial use back in 1856 when the one-cent magenta was printed. Back in those days, they used woodcuts or metal engravings for illustrations, not screened illustrations such as this. The one-cent magenta was printed by letterpress—typography, as it's sometimes called. The type on the one-cent magenta was set by hand and surrounded by a rule, a printer's term for a line. The ship is a printer's stock decorative cut. Your one-cent magenta was printed in the twentieth century. You can see the dots clearly enough."

Woody put a magnifying glass to the stamp, then looked up sheepishly. He knew I was right. Did he feel foolish? I would have. But then humility wasn't Woody's strong suit. While I looked on— and without another word to me—he picked up the phone and called New York.

"Woody B. Goode here," he said, flicking the stock card against his thumb as he spoke. Listen, I've had an expert out here look at that stamp, and he doesn't think it's genuine."

Suddenly I was an expert, I mused. Only moments before I had been a know-nothing.

"On closer inspection, I think I have to concur with his opinion." Woody didn't sound the slightest bit embarrassed for having jumped to the conclusion that he had a genuine stamp. The one-cent magenta is probably the most reproduced stamp in existence. Reproductions range from magazine illustrations to promotional facsimiles.

You should have put it under a glass to begin with, I thought. Besides, the stamp is in perfect condition, looks like it was printed yesterday. You should have known better.

"I just wanted to let you know," Woody said into the phone. "Naturally, I won't be sending it now."

How skillful Woody was at putting a good face on an embarrassing situation. What must the unseen person on the other end of the line think? I wondered if he were as amused as I was.

"Okay, thanks for your trouble." Woody hung up, then looked at me.

I couldn't hide my amusement.

But my amusement didn't bother the irrepressible Woody one bit. He shrugged, as if nothing unusual had happened, and said, "Oh, well, easy come, easy go."

A GHOST STORY

"Do you believe in ghosts?" Sherman Lindy asked, right out of the blue. It was an unusual question coming from Sherman, but perhaps I shouldn't have been surprised. You see, Sherman Lindy is probably the closest I'll ever come to knowing a true genius.

"No," I answered, wondering what prompted the question. Then voicing my curiosity, "Do you?"

"Let's say I'm keeping an open mind. Which brings me to the point. How would you like to sit in on a seance?"

I didn't know what to say.

My visit to Lindy Engineering that afternoon had begun routinely enough. I had brought a $2.60 Zeppelin plate block for Sherman Lindy's consideration. It was the last one needed to complete his set. I hoped I would make a sale, even though the plate block wasn't quite as nice as the two lower values I'd sold him. Then suddenly, the question of a seance.

For a long, uncomfortable moment I hesitated, struggled for an answer, unable to decide whether to accept or decline. My impulse was to decline, but I didn't want to offend Sherman. He was a good customer, and besides, I liked him. So I groped for a graceful excuse, but none would stand and volunteer.

"I hope you'll say yes," Sherman prodded.

I searched his face for any clue about what lay behind his extraordinary invitation. But it was as inscrutable as the Sphinx's.

We got together at Sherman Lindy's office Friday afternoons, every other week or so, whenever I had something new to offer. I didn't normally make house calls to sell stamps, but in Sherman's case, I made an exception. I did so because not only was he a serious stamp collector with the financial ability to indulge his hobby, but because Sherman Lindy was one of the most fascinating men I have ever known.

No matter what the subject—science, art, music, history, philosophy, psychology, economics—he could speak knowledgeably about it. I don't recall a subject, with the possible exception of philately, about which I knew more than Sherman.

Sherman was one of those rare individuals who combined the mental traits of prodigious memory with lightning-quick intellect. He used his incisive intellect—which could cut every bit as effortlessly and seamlessly as a beam of laser light—to hone information-in-the-rough into perfectly faceted bodies of fact. He shaped them expertly until they sparkled bright and gemlike.

Sherman liked to ponder the big "ifs": the creation of the universe; the chemical nature of the origin of life; the physics of subatomic particles; the grand unified theory. An afternoon with Sherman was pure intellectual exhilaration, like going back to college, but without the homework and exams.

Sherman had interesting observations on philately, too. No use talking to him about the importance of watermarks or perforation varieties. "Stamps interest me because of their beauty," he once remarked. "That's why I collect them. Take the Washington-Franklin series. The designs are identical, which contributes cohesiveness. The colors differ, which contributes esthetic appeal. Arrayed together you have symmetry and beauty . . . and that's the magic of it.

"Perforations and watermarks are irrelevant, and in no way integral to my esthetic appreciation of the form. I don't collect them because I won't allow myself to fall victim to the tyranny of the irrelevant."

"But perforation and watermark varieties are universally recognized—" I started to say, cringing at Sherman's philatelic heresy.

"Nevertheless, irrelevant," Sherman interrupted, as if correcting a slow, uncomprehending student. "My goal is to obtain stamps that appeal to me . . . to appreciate the esthetics. I have no interest in assembling every possible production combination and permutation. To me, at least, such an exercise is mindless and completely extraneous to my enjoyment of the hobby. Again, that's my own personal opinion."

I argued no further. It wouldn't have done any good. Besides, philately should be a joy, not a regimen. Live and let live. Let each individual pursue the hobby in whatever fashion pleases him.

Sherman Lindy was in his early thirties when I first met him in the early 1970s. He had a boyish look about him and a quiet demeanor that could easily be mistaken for shyness. I'm not sure what a genius is supposed to look like, but Sherman's appearance contrasted sharply with the searing brilliance of his mind. He looked average in every way: average height, average weight, and casual clothes that looked slightly too large for him. He wore his brown hair functionally short. Had it been longer, it would have appeared disheveled and alive with the electricity of intellect, like Einstein's or Beethoven's.

Lindy Engineering occupied a nondescript, modern prefab building in an industrial park. A rail spur sidled up to the rear. On the inside, it was much brighter, due in no small part to Juliet Schonbrun. Juliet was Sherman Lindy's receptionist and girl Friday. She greeted visitors from her desk just inside the front door.

Juliet, whom I judged to be in her mid-twenties, reminded me of a sunny day: warm, pleasant and cheerful. She was a beautiful woman, tall, blond, and athletic, statuesque in an informal way. She walked with natural, effortless grace. She looked as if she had just strolled off a California beach, turning every pair of eyes along the way. Juliet's personality could best be summed up by the phrase "Let the sun shine in!" from the pop song "Aquarius."

Juliet was responsible for the light, airy motif of the reception area, its exuberantly colored furnishings, the news and general interest magazines that—in addition to purely technical journals—awaited visitors. A copy of *Your Horoscope Today* stood beside *The Secretarial Handbook* on Juliet's desk. A couple of wildly colorful, abstract-patterned wall hangings further brightened the reception area. Sherman referred to them as products of an undisciplined mind adrift in a sea of chaos. But Juliet liked them and paid no attention to his opinion.

In contrast to the reception area, Sherman's second-floor office looked drab. It was windowless, isolated from the environmental cues of the outside world—the sun in transit and the weather. The office measured about thirty feet long by twenty feet wide. Cork paneling covered the walls. Pinned to the cork were hundreds of pieces of paper: notes on quadrille paper, paper napkins, backs of envelopes, and myriad scraps of paper. They included scientific notations, schematic diagrams, clippings from magazines and newspapers, calendars, and take-out menus. A long, built-in counter ran the length of one wall. It was cluttered with electronic gadgetry: soldering irons, circuit boards, and rainbow-colored wires. Countertops along other walls contained compartmented bins for the bulk storage of transistors, resistors, and other electronic components, the building blocks of Sherman's inventions.

Sherman had made several million dollars inventing and selling a missile component to the Defense Department, a component that the big budget research teams and established contractors had been unable to perfect. He had quietly created it in his informal Tom Swift laboratory, and he was justifiably proud of that.

Early on, I learned that Juliet was fascinated by the paranormal, by elusive concepts that lurked in half-light at the edge of the glow cast by the firelight of knowledge.

One Friday, while waiting for Sherman, who had not yet returned from an errand away from the office, Juliet asked, "What's your sign, Mr. Datz?"

"Gemini, I think. I'm afraid I'm really not into horoscopes."

"Neither is Sherman. Says astrology's a lot of superstitious nonsense."

I was amused. I could visualize Sherman trying to explain there could be no possible scientific significance to the fact that Jupiter might be aligned with Mars, as it applied to the affairs of any given human being.

"Mr. Lindy *is* extremely knowledgeable," I remarked.

"Yes. I think he's a genius," Juliet said sincerely. "But that doesn't mean he knows everything. Astrology's been around for thousands of years. There must be a reason."

"It's beyond me," I said, not wanting to get involved in a subject I cared little about. Fortuitously, at that moment Sherman strolled in the front door.

"I hope you're not bothering Steve with all that astrology stuff," he said. Diplomatically, he had not used the word *nonsense*. "C'mon up," he said, walking by me. "I'm anxious to see what philatelic treasures you've brought today." I rose and followed him up the stairs to his office.

"Juliet is a wonderful woman," Sherman said, as we walked to his office. "I couldn't get along without her. I've tried to explain to her that mysticism has no scientific, no factual basis. But it doesn't do any good. Still, I guess everyone's entitled to his or her own opinion, whether it has merit or not. Have a seat. Let's see what you've got for me," Sherman said that day.

I had brought a 65-cent Zeppelin plate block, the first he would need to complete the set of three. He liked it and bought it.

Months later, on the day of the seance, I would offer him the high value of the set.

"I hope you'll say yes," Sherman said, bringing me back to the present and the question of the seance.

"It all sounds rather mysterious," I said. "What's going on, anyway?"

"The seance is for Juliet."

"For Juliet? But I thought you didn't believe in that sort of stuff."

"I don't, but Juliet has gone a bit overboard with all this crackpot mysticism. She went to a paranormal convention a couple of weeks ago. One of those affairs where those without scientific background or intellectual discipline speak authoritatively on pseudo-scientific subjects to the gullible, to those with marginal knowledge or intelligence. As far as I'm concerned, it's just a racket."

It was unusual to hear so much acid in Sherman's voice.

"At the meeting," Sherman continued, "she met a man who claims to be some kind of minister, a self-proclaimed guru of the inexplicable. I don't remember the name of the church. I'm sure it's not a real church.

"Anyway, this he's been filling her head with all sorts of nonsense about spirit communication and parallel dimensions. He's been holding seminars—if you can call them that—for people who're interested in the paranormal. And his expertise doesn't come cheap. He charges hefty fees.

"Now don't get me wrong," Sherman said. "Intellectual curiosity is a wonderful thing, and everyone is certainly entitled to his opinion, but I've got a feeling this guy's nothing more than a con man."

I'd never seen Sherman so agitated.

"Worse yet, Juliet's beginning to believe some of this hokum—astral projection, communication with unreincarnated human spirits, with alien entities, with beings from parallel dimensions, you name it. She doesn't realize that he's making it up as he goes along.

"If you want to believe in that stuff, okay," Sherman said. "But when you start passing fantasy off as fact and charging for it, that's fraud. Poor Juliet has neither the education nor background to enable her to distinguish scientific fact from palpable nonsense. This guru-minister—or whatever he is—is taking advantage of her, and it irks the hell out of me!"

Fire danced in Sherman's eyes.

"Juliet respects my scientific background, my knowledge and intelligence," he said.

Sherman was, in fact, being modest. Juliet was in awe of his prodigious intellect, but she mistook his out-of-hand dismissal of mysticism for narrow-mindedness rather than analytical conclusion. She was devoted to Sherman, not just because of her job or a sense of duty, but, it seemed, for something beyond that.

And whether he realized it or not, Sherman was devoted to her and extremely protective of her. That much was apparent from his reaction to her forays into the paranormal.

"So," Sherman continued, "I'm holding the seance for Juliet's sake. To be objective, to investigate this unknown that intrigues her so much. I hope it will help her see the truth. And, I've invited her witch-doctor friend to attend.

That surprised me, but I didn't interrupt.

"I've been boning up on the spirit world all week," he said. "I'm going to hold it in the conference room. I've asked my whole crew to attend." He smiled a slightly odd smile. Did I detect mischief dancing in those oddly enthusiastic eyes? Or was it my imagination?

"I'm not much on seances," I said, casting about for a diplomatic way to excuse myself, but Sherman wasn't about to let the matter drop.

"C'mon, Steve, where's your intellectual curiosity?" he prodded. "We're on a great scientific adventure here, a quest for truth. And truth we shall have. Besides, I'm going to buy your stamps," he said, putting the $2.60 Zepp plate block into his desk drawer to emphasize that the deal was done. "So humor a good customer and enjoy yourself at the same time. Who knows, we might just contact some spirits and change the way man perceives the universe! What do you say?"

How could I refuse? "Okay," I said.

"Wonderful! We'll get started just as soon as Matheson arrives. He's Juliet's voodoo buddy, calls himself *Reverend* Matheson."

We assembled in a windowless conference room dominated by a large circular table capable of seating a dozen people. On Juliet's left sat a thin, clean-shaven man who introduced himself as Reverend Matheson. Sherman sat on Juliet's right, and I sat on Sherman's right. Reverend Matheson—if indeed he were a minister—wore a clerical collar and appeared to be in his late thirties. He smiled affably, apparently unaware of Sherman's virulent skepticism and considerable intellectual muscle.

Sherman's employees ringed the remaining seats: Bob, the shop foreman, five workers, and Sylvia, the bookkeeping clerk. What must they have thought? Holding a seance seemed silly enough, except that it was Sherman's idea, and one could only guess what might spring from the unfathomable depths of his mind. Bob and the crew joked good-naturedly. Matheson smiled, perhaps amused, perhaps nervous.

"Ladies and gentlemen," Sherman began, "we're gathered here in the spirit of scientific discovery, to delve, to probe, to explore the unknown. Perhaps to touch upon one of the great mysteries of the universe.

"As you know, I'm a skeptic. I must be shown facts in order to be persuaded." Sherman scanned the assembled faces, as spoke. "But never let it be said that I don't have an open mind. And that's why we're here today, to embark on a scientific experiment.

"I've done a little research on seances recently, and I think I've grasped the basics, so if you'll bear with me, we'll get started.

"Bob, Steve, would you please assist me? Each of you tie one of my hands with a piece of rope," he said, extending his wrists and handing each of us a piece of white clothesline. "Tie them securely. Juliet, when they've finished, wrap a piece of masking tape around each of the knots." It took only a moment to secure Sherman's wrists. Juliet wrapped tape around the knots. "Bob, Steve, please initial the tape." We did. Then Sherman crossed his arms straightjacket style and said, "Now, please tie the ends of the ropes to the back legs of the chair. Also, tie my feet to the front chair legs. When they've finished, any of you are welcome to inspect their work." No one bothered. Like a man in a straightjacket, Sherman was securely bound.

"Now, all of you join hands, and place them on the table," Sherman instructed. "Don't let go for any reason, and make no sudden movements. That's important. Do you understand?"

Everyone nodded and joined hands. Viewed from above, the joined, outstretched hands resembled, with kaleidoscopic symmetry, a giant snowflake.

"If you let go, the synergy of the spirit field we hope to create may be disrupted. So, please, whatever happens, don't let go.

"I will serve as guide. If we contact any spirits—which I doubt we will—it's important to keep our wits and investigate in an orderly fashion. Is that clear?"

Heads bobbed in unison.

"Okay then, I think we're about ready. Bob, please kill the lights."

The conference room went black instantly. Normally, as one's eyes grow accustomed to darkness, faint pinpoints of light become visible. Stray light from adjacent rooms sneaks in under doors or through cracks in windowsills. But the conference room at Lindy Engineering was devoid of light. The blackness was absolute and impenetrable.

"I will now attempt to summon the spirits," Sherman said. "Spirits, if you can hear me, show yourselves. We are wayfarers in an uncertain universe seeking contact with kindred spirits. We have open minds and open hearts. Make us aware of your presence. I implore you. Let us, who would welcome knowledge of your existence, see you and hear you. Come forward from the vast, unexplored regions of the cosmos, wherever you may reside. Come forward and meet fellow beings." Sherman's voice rose. His entreaties assumed an urgent, disembodied, otherworldly quality, and they sent a cold caterpillar of a shiver crawling up my spine.

"Manifest yourselves, spirits, wherever you may be. Hear my voice and come to us. We have open minds. You will be among friends. Share your presence and your secrets with us. We have many questions. Please, if you can hear me, come to this place."

The entreaty went on for several minutes. Sherman's giving it his best shot, I thought. After this is over, Juliet should have no doubts about the futility of sitting in a dark room talking to nonexistent entities.

"Spirits, I implore you . . . manifest yourselves. Give us a sign of your existence."

Suddenly, we all gasped collectively. A small, cold, yellowish-white light hovered near the ceiling, then moved slowly around the room. It dipped and soared, dancing in the blackness, then zoomed madly over our heads, circling the room in an instant.

I couldn't believe my eyes. The shiver that Sherman's incantations had sent up my spine turned glacier-cold. My mouth went dry. I tasted something metallic, adrenaline-flavored. Reflexively, I held my breath, and I could have sworn that even my heart paused. For a long moment, I dangled in the blackness, in the vacuum between complete awe and abject fear.

The light was cold and tenuous. It cast no illumination. I couldn't see anyone or anything. Yet it was bright in its own peculiar way, as if light flowed into it rather than emanating from it.

"I see you, my light-friend," Sherman said. "You have come from somewhere beyond our knowing. We are curious and eager to know more about you."

But before he could go any further, the light winked out.

"Did you see that?" a voice whispered.

"Yes," came a hushed reply, then another.

"It was as big as a grapefruit," a voice said.

Others piped in. "I thought it was about the size of a quarter."

It could have been any size. There was no reference against which to measure it.

"Did you see the way it zoomed? Zero to light speed in an instant?"

"It's evidence of the great interdimensional spirit world," Matheson piped up.

"Do you smell anything?"

"Yes, what an odd odor."

"It's ozone," Sherman said. A light fragrance filled the room. It was oddly sweet and bitter at once. I had smelled it before, somewhere, but couldn't place it.

"Oh, my God," Juliet said, "something's touching my hand. It's freezing cold."

"What is it?" Sherman asked.

"It's feels like ice water . . . but it isn't. It's not wet. It feels wet, but it's not. It's like it's there . . . but it isn't." Juliet struggled to articulate the sensation, but words eluded her.

"I feel it, too," Matheson chimed in. "Icy cold. Something flowed over our hands, like a liquid without substance. I can feel it, but when I try to rub it between my fingers, nothing's there."

"Odd indeed," Sherman muttered.

"And there's a cold spot on the table," Matheson continued. "You feel it, don't you, Juliet?"

"Yes, it's right next to our hands. The table feels like it's been flash frozen."

Then Sherman spoke, taking control of the situation, "Spirit—whoever you are, whatever you are—have you left us? Can you still hear me?" With that, there came a rumbling from the ceiling, as if the suspended tiles were rippling, bouncing. Sounds came first from one place, then another, from every part of the room. Then silence followed.

"Spirit, if you hear me, if you can understand me, signify by knocking once for yes and twice for no."

From the ceiling came a knock, as if someone had tapped a tile just hard enough to lift it slightly off its suspension track.

"Good," Sherman said. Then a single, gentle knock came from the center of the table, and an instant later, still another from the far corner of the room, as if the entity were everywhere at once.

"Amazing," Matheson said, "The spirit can move from one place to another instantly, unfettered by the physical laws of our universe or our dimension."

"Let's try to find out more about this thing," Sherman said, interrupting Matheson's musings. "We've established that the entity can hear us, can signal yes or no."

I sat in the molasses-like darkness, dumbfounded. The reality of the universe as I knew it had suddenly been pulled out from under my feet. The eeriness of the inky room and its otherworldly inhabitant would have spooked me had not Sherman remained so composed and objective. His voice was devoid of fear, and to me that was remarkable because he was bound, hand and foot, to a chair.

"Let's play twenty questions," Sherman said. Then, surprisingly, "Reverend Matheson, you've had more experience at this than I have. Would you like to question the entity?"

"Why, yes. Thank you," Matheson said, sounding flattered by the deference shown him.

"Are you a spirit?"

One knock from a ceiling tile: yes.

"Are you from earth?"

One knock, again from a ceiling tile.

"Were you once a human being?"

One knock, this time from the center of the table.

"Did you live near here?"

One knock, from the corner ceiling.

"Did you die near here?"

One knock, this time from the far wall.

"Did you live in our time?"

Two knocks, a no, from the opposite side of the room.

"He moves around a lot," Sherman noted. The others sat as silently as the room was black.

"Did you live fifty years ago?" Matheson continued.

Two knocks: no.

"Earlier than fifty years?"

One knock: yes.

"Earlier than a hundred years ago?"

Yes.

"Absolutely amazing! We're talking to the spirit of a man who lived before the 1870s, a century ago," Matheson said, his hushed voice filled with the kind of awe one might experience in the presence of the President or the Queen of England.

"Were you a pioneer?" Sherman asked.

Two knocks. Then, one knock.

"Sounds like a maybe," Sherman said.

"Did you come out during the gold rush?" Sherman asked.

One knock: yes.

"Denver was the staging point for prospectors during the gold rush of 1859," Sherman said. "Before that, Colorado was largely unsettled. Perhaps he was part of the gold rush. Were you a prospector?"

A single knock answered Sherman's question.

"Sorry for interrupting," Sherman said.

"That's okay," Matheson replied. "We learned that he died near here. Let's explore that some more. Did you die a natural death?"

Two knocks: no.

"A violent death?"

One knock, very loud, from the center of the table.

"Were you killed by Indians?"

Two knocks, again very loud, from the ceiling. The tiles banged and rattled with the force of the blows.

"Must have been unpleasant," Sherman muttered.

Another loud single knock, again from the ceiling tiles.

"Were you shot?"

This time two very loud bangs from the center of the table, as if someone had pounded it with a heavy fist.

"Stabbed?"

Two more loud crashes from the ceiling tiles. The atmosphere of the room tensed. The restless rage or torment of the unseen entity made itself felt.

"I don't think he likes talking about it," Sherman said.

"Were you hanged?" Matheson blurted out, his voice eager, like a hound that had suddenly picked up a fresh and irresistibly strong scent.

One enormous, violent bang reverberated from the center of the table. We could feel it ripple through our hands.

"For murder?" Matheson pressed.

Two severe blows crashed overhead.

"For robbery?"

The table shuddered under the impact of two more forceful blows.

"Horse thievery?" Sherman offered.

One blow, then two.

"I think I've got it," Sherman said. "You were hanged for horse thievery." There was a firm, but comparatively gentle knock on the table. "But you didn't do it. You were hanged unjustly!"

Immediately, a violent crash rocked the tiles above our heads. And then the table began to shake and bounce, literally off its footing. It was a heavy table with a single center support made of metal, a fact that made its sudden convulsions all the more unnerving.

A plastic tumbler flew across the room and bounced off the far wall, immediately followed by a flurry of objects crashing and bouncing off walls, as if everything in the room not fastened down had suddenly become airborne. We couldn't see anything in the liquid blackness, only hear and feel the energetic, terrifying rampage, as the entity unleashed its pent-up fury, fury that had festered for more than a century. Papers, pencils, plastic glasses, books, anything loose, flew through the raven-black void in a frenzy, as if propelled by a swirling tornado, yet the air itself was as still and unmoving as death.

It was not a movie, not a play. It was horrifyingly real. The noise and the confusion struck absolute, stark terror into me. I couldn't move, couldn't even think of what to do next. In that fearful moment, I suddenly knew exactly how a rabbit felt, frozen in the headlights of an oncoming truck.

"It grabbed my shoulder!" Bob shrieked, his normally calm voice suddenly high-pitched with panic. *"Oh, my dear God, it's grabbed me! I'm getting out of here!"*

"Easy, Bob. Just turn on the light." Sherman's reassuring voice instructed calmly from the blackness. He was completely in control.

The light came on, and the room was suddenly familiar again. The infinite blackness, the unfathomable unknown was magically gone. The universe again became recognizable and manageable.

"I think you made it mad," Sherman said, looking at Matheson, who appeared even more white-faced than the rest of us. Objects that had flown through the darkness littered the room. The ceiling tiles were intact. Sherman was bound tightly in his chair. Bob stood at the light switch near the door, looking a bit sheepish.

"Sorry," he said. "Something grabbed my shoulder . . . something very strong. It scared the hell out of me."

"That's okay," Sherman said. "Will someone please untie me?"

I reached over to loosen his bonds, noting that the initialed tape was still intact.

"I think we could all use a drink," Sherman said, removing the last of the rope from his wrists. The congregation murmured in agreement, perhaps more eager to leave the room, than to have the drink.

Our small band—we outworld explorers—filed into the employee lounge, made ourselves drinks, and took seats at the rectangular common table. Sherman sat at its head. Bob and one of his crew hadn't arrived yet.

"What'd you think of that?" Sherman asked, sipping a Jack Daniels.

"I wouldn't have believed it if I hadn't seen," I said. Murmurs acknowledged that all shared the sentiment.

"I think it proves that there are forces in the universe we don't understand," Matheson said. "There are other dimensions, other beings, beings without substance, realms we can't begin to imagine."

"Amen," Sherman said, sipping his drink casually. Did I detect the faintest glimmer of smugness in his tone?

"There are, indeed, forces we don't understand," Sherman said, as if reiterating the painfully obvious. "We don't completely understand magnetic force or the weak force—binder of atoms. We don't completely understand gravity. But we can hypothesize mathematically about the existence of gravitons, top quarks, and tau neutrinos. We can do that because natural phenomena obey the laws of physics. That's how we learn about the universe."

"But there are other forces, beings from realms we don't understand—"

"They would, of necessity, behave according to natural laws," Sherman interrupted. "We should be able to observe, measure and analyze them."

"They may, or they may not," Matheson said. "Entities may come from a parallel universe or a dimension so strange we can't even imagine it."

"Then how do they hear us?" Sherman asked. "Do they have ears? If they have no substance, how do they interact with physical objects in our universe?"

"They may operate according to rules of their own space-time continuum."

"But they were in our room, in our space-time continuum. Therefore, they must—I stress *must*—behave according to the physical laws of our universe." Then, "Do you even know what a space-time continuum is? Do you know what a dimension is? A parallel universe? Or are you just enamored of the words?"

Matheson paused. The exchange had begun to take on the flavor of confrontation. He didn't answer the question, but neither did he appear unbalanced by it.

"How do you explain the events we just witnessed?" he demanded.

"I'm sure there's an explanation," Sherman said. "I'm also sure it lies within the scope of our present understanding of the universe, not out in left field, in some imaginary parallel dimension."

Just then Bob and Dave walked into the room. "Had to check out the conference room, Boss," Bob said. "You're a genius with gadgets. Thought you might have rigged that little show for us."

Sherman wrinkled his brow in mock dismay, looking pained at the notion that someone might doubt him.

"What did you find?" Sherman asked.

"Nothing. The room checked out clean. No wires, no devices, no lights, nothing." Sherman continued to look pained. "No offense, Boss, just thought you might be playing a joke."

"Maybe we just imagined it," Sherman suggested. "Group hysteria, mass hypnosis."

"I didn't imagine the spook that grabbed my shoulder," Bob said emphatically. "It was strong. I don't know what it was . . . and I don't want to find out." We all chuckled.

"Odd that our mysterious guest couldn't articulate sound," Sherman said.

"Not at all," Matheson countered. "It may have been a plasma entity—"

"Do you know what plasma is?" Sherman asked, straightening up in his chair, looking directly at Matheson. Before he could answer, Sherman replied, "It's a state of matter, like a solid, a liquid, or a gas, but in a very high temperature state. So hot, in fact, that electrons become disassociated—stripped—from atomic nuclei and swim, together with positive ions, in a super-hot, essentially gaseous soup. The same soup that exists in thermonuclear reactions. The sun is composed of matter in the plasma state. Plasma would have instantly incinerated the room!"

"Well, I used the term plasma in the paranormal sense—"

"If you're going to play at scientific investigation, it might behoove you to have a rudimentary understanding of the terminology you're bandying about, if not the underlying principles." Like a white-hot, solar prominence, Sherman's comments flared, searing Matheson's ears. The rest of us could feel the heat.

"You may not understand what you witnessed, but I wouldn't approach it on a pseudo-scientific basis. I wouldn't attempt to explain it using borrowed, bastardized scientific terminology, words you don't even know the meaning of. I wouldn't fantasize, then couch my mental meanderings in a lot of mystical mumbo-jumbo, as if they had some basis in fact."

Sherman blazed away. "Approach the unknown scientifically. Study it according to scientific disciplines. Then, if you can explain what you've discovered, you'll render a valuable service to your fellow man."

Matheson remained silent.

"On the other hand," Sherman said, looking first at Juliet, then at Matheson, "there are those who don't want answers. Pseudo-scientific dilettantes perfectly content to be mystified. They're infatuated with the inexplicable, exhilarated by the unknown. They revel in it. In fact, they prefer the unknown to remain unknown, so it can continue as an object of speculation. They enjoy the quest for esoteric knowledge, enjoy masquerading as zealous—if incompetent—truth seekers.

"And there's another breed," Sherman continued, now fixing his gaze on Matheson, "a predatory breed who feeds on the ignorance of the dilettante. They set themselves up as authorities on the paranormal. They extract money in exchange for plausible-sounding yet deceptive nonsense. They're nothing more than a bunch of con men.

"Yes," Sherman said, glancing at the others, "you witnessed a real phenomenon. No question about it. And just as surely as you saw and heard it, it has an explanation. At the moment, you don't know what it is. If you're truly interested in understanding a phenomenon, then approach it with the discipline of a professional, not the wild-eyed passion of a dilettante. I guarantee that all things with a basis in fact are explainable."

"How would you explain the events we witnessed?" Matheson challenged.

"I'm not going to try today. Perhaps another day. I do know one thing. The entity became extremely violent when you questioned it. Perhaps it took a personal dislike to you. I don't think I'd be too quick to fool around with something I don't understand, especially something with a propensity for violence. Who knows what it's capable of? What it would do next time? I'd be very careful if I were you," Sherman said, looking directly at Matheson.

Matheson remained silent, perhaps chastened, perhaps unwilling to provoke Sherman further. There was little doubt who would emerge the winner in an intellectual duel. Juliet looked uncomfortable and embarrassed.

"I must leave now," Sherman said, rising. "I have some things to attend to." Then, surveying the assembled faces, he said, "Someday you'll have an explanation for what you witnessed today. And that explanation will conform to the laws of the natural universe."

And with that, Sherman Lindy turned and left the room.

A long, heavy moment of silence followed. Everyone seemed lost in thought. Then Bob, ever ready with a quip, said, "I hope this doesn't mean we're going to have to work in a haunted building."

"Maybe our spirit friend won't bother us as long as we don't bring up the hanging," Dave, one the technicians, said.

"I've never been so scared," Sylvia said, crossing herself. "I'll be looking over my shoulder from now on."

"I never believed in ghosts before," Dave said. "But I'll never scoff at them again." his remarks seemed to echo everyone's feelings.

"Did you see how calm Sherman was?" Sylvia said. Juliet nodded. She had noticed. "The man's got a brain sharp as a razor, and he's cool as an iceberg."

Then Matheson spoke, having held his tongue long enough. "We witnessed something profound, something extraordinary today. Something science and the so-called experts can't explain," he said, again assuming his self-important role as guru of the paranormal. The sarcasm in his tone was evident and disturbing. What he had been afraid to say in Sherman's presence, he now said behind his back. "They don't have a monopoly on knowledge. They don't know everything. They've no right to be so damn arrogant!" His voice rose. He made no attempt to hide his contempt.

"Sherman may not know everything," Juliet said, suddenly bristling, "but he's a lot smarter than any of us will ever be. He's a good boss. A good and honest man. I'm not going to sit here and listen to anyone make remarks about him behind his back."

Matheson, somewhat chastened by Juliet's outburst, stood. "I can see, dear people, that the time has come for me to leave. Thank you for inviting me," he said to Juliet, trying to regain his dignity. She nodded but didn't speak. Matheson turned to leave.

"Don't let the Boogie Man get you," Bob quipped. A barely audible chuckle rustled through the room. Matheson neither stopped nor acknowledged the remark.

Matheson's departure acted as a catalyst. The others, too, rose, gathered coats, filtered into the reception area, said their goodnights, and left.

I'd almost forgotten that I'd left my attaché case in Sherman's office. Although I didn't want to disturb him, neither did I want to leave without it. I climbed the stairs. His office door was ajar. I knocked and cracked it open a little more.

"I just need to get my attaché case," I said.

"Sure, come on in." He looked up from his work, the bright, pale light from his fluorescent desk lamp giving his face an otherworldly appearance. He rose and came around the desk to meet me. "Say, I hope the seance didn't disturb you too much."

"No," I lied.

"I did it for Juliet's benefit. To show her the absurdity, the chicanery of that voodoo charlatan and all his mystical mumbo-jumbo."

"But you proved Matheson's point. You proved that spirits exist," I said, amazed to hear myself make such a statement.

Sherman took my arm and cocked his head back in a hearty chuckle. "All is not as it seems, my friend," he said. "Sometimes you can't trust even your senses."

He contrived it! flashed into my head. *But how?* Bob checked the room thoroughly. The light, the cold spots, the ozone, the disembodied rattlings and rumblings, the frenzied flying objects—how could he fake those effects?

Sherman grinned the maddening grin of one in on an inside joke. "I did it all," he said, smiling from ear to ear.

"But how? You were tied to the chair. I tied you myself! Matheson tied the other hand. The knots were solid."

He chuckled. Then after a moment, "That's what made it so plausible."

I stood there, blank-faced.

"I'm sorry, my friend," he continued, "but it was all a deliciously wonderful hoax. Did you see Matheson's face?" Sherman Lindy was immensely pleased with himself.

"But how?"

"Harry Houdini. It's all in his book. I got it from the library. You know, Houdini didn't believe in the supernatural, either. He attended hundreds of seances during his lifetime and exposed them as frauds. He never found a genuine medium, never found a genuine case of spirit contact. His book explains the tricks that mediums use. I simply borrowed a few. They're so simple, it took only about fifteen minutes to master them. Turn your back for a moment."

I turned away, still reeling from the turn of events.

"Okay, I'm ready." He had returned to his chair. "First, you tied me up." He held one end of a long piece of rope in each hand. The other ends hung loosely at his sides. "Observe. You have tied my wrists. Now, I'll cross my arms so you can secure them straightjacket style behind my back."

Sherman demonstrated Houdini's technique: thumbs from opposing hands caught the strands as they crossed in front of him and pushed them back toward the elbow of the wrist to which they were tied. Rather than being tied straightjacket style, the trailing ends were actually fastened to chair legs on the same side as each bound wrist. By simply unfolding his arms, Sherman was free. He had instant full use of his hands. The motion of the crossing wrists happened so quickly, so smoothly, it was impossible to detect unless you were watching for it.

"Amazing!" I said.

"The instant the lights were out, I was free to do whatever I wanted."

From inside his shirt he extracted a carpenter's wooden folding ruler.

"Spray painted it black," he said, unfolding it section by section. "Manifest yourself, spirit," he said, tapping the extended end against the ceiling tile. "One knock for yes, two knocks for no."

We both laughed. From his pocket he extracted a small circular object attached to a rubber band. "Piece of felt painted with luminescent paint," he said, attaching it to the end of the extended ruler. He moved it around. The secret of the phantom light was revealed. "The interesting thing about total darkness is that, when deprived of reference points, one's senses can only estimate the size of an object. Remember, to some it appeared the size of a grapefruit, while to others, the size of a quarter—its actual size. The group's comments, their disagreement over its size only added to the ambiance of the show."

"And the ozone? The cold spots?"

"Ether." He extracted a spray can from his desk drawer. "It's the main constituent of carburetor quick-start fluid." He held the spray can's nozzle to the neck of a small glass bottle. In five seconds the bottle was filled with colorless liquid. "Ether has a very low evaporation point. It's highly volatile, and has a pronounced odor. I gambled that no one would recognize it. I even made the comment about ozone, again guessing that no one knew what ozone smelled like. And they bought it. The power of suggestion.

"Ether evaporates so quickly, it flash chills whatever it's in contact with."

He poured a small puddle of the clear liquid on the desktop. It was gone in an instant.

"Now, feel the spot." I did. It was ice cold. "I poured ether toward where I thought Juliet's and Matheson's hands might be, and I must have aimed well. They felt the liquid, but by the time they tried to rub it between their fingers, it was gone—evaporated. It's a devilishly strange sensation."

I tried it, and it was. You felt the liquid, but you couldn't hold it.

"And the flying objects? You tossed them."

"Yup. Made sure beforehand that there were plastic glasses behind me on the counter, and paperclips, pencils, light stuff that would make plenty of noise, create a lot of confusion, but cause no harm to anyone in the event they were hit."

Then he rocked his desk with one hand and bumped the ceiling tiles with the ruler held in his other. "Creates quite an illusion in a dark room."

"You had *me* scared to death," I said. "I left your spookfest convinced that ghosts exist. And what about the hand that grabbed Bob?"

"Sheer luck. The ruler bent in my frenzied poking and thrashing."

He demonstrated. A section flexed downward under whipsawing movement.

"Apparently it hit Bob on the shoulder, because that's when he shouted that he'd been grabbed. I thought the game was up. What I didn't realize was how greatly darkness can disorient a person. He didn't know it was a ruler. He was so suggestible, so immersed in the events of the moment, that he imagined something actually grabbed him. His startled comment was a beautiful, spontaneous touch. I barely had time to get the ruler folded and into my shirt, and return my arms to their tied position before he reached the lights."

"Amazing!" I said. "Absolutely amazing!" The seance had completely fooled me. In the darkness, amid the noise and confusion, it had been utterly, terrifyingly real.

"It's incredible the degree to which the mind can be influenced and tricked," Sherman said. "With the aid of unsuspecting victims' own suggestibility, it's easy for phony mediums to stage successful seances. And the power of suggestion works even more persuasively on those predisposed to believe in the occult. The medium performs a few parlor tricks, controls the patter, suggests what's occurring, and the unsuspecting, cued by their senses, buy it. After a few minutes, the mind stops evaluating sensory input in the context of its normal environment and, instead, overwhelmed by unusual phenomena, interprets sensory input according to the path of least resistance—the medium's suggestions."

"Are you going to tell Juliet?"

"Of course . . . but not right away. Please don't say anything."

"I won't," I assured him.

Over the years, I made many house calls to Lindy Engineering and sold many wonderful stamps to Sherman Lindy. I never spoke about the seance to Juliet, nor after that October day, did she ever again mention astrology to me. On the fifteenth of June in the year following the seance, Sherman and Juliet were married. They've been very happy together ever since.

And although I've not heard of Matheson since, he may well still be making the rounds of paranormal conventions.

MORE GOOD READING
BY STEPHEN R. DATZ

TOP DOLLAR PAID!
ISBN 0-88219-022-9

The best selling book about buying and selling stamps. It's two books in one: a concise factual guide, and an entertaining, revealing behind-the-scenes narrative about the real-life world of stamp dealing written by a dealer with decades of experience. Included is a chapter relating Datz's experiences appraising President Gerald R. Ford's stamp collection and arranging for its sale at auction. Critically acclaimed, it's an absolute must-read for anyone who buys, collects, or invests, as well as anyone thinking about selling a stamp collection and getting top dollar.

STAMP COLLECTING
ISBN 0-88219-030-X

Stamp Collecting contains everything you need to know to get started. Written by long-time stamp dealer and philatelic author Stephen R. Datz, *Stamp Collecting* covers the essentials in a series of convenient, easy-to-use chapters. Datz makes use of his experience and intimate knowledge of the hobby to explain to go about obtaining the maximum enjoyment from philately. Profuse illustrations augment the text. Perfect for anyone interested in discovering the fun of the World's Most Popular Hobby!

ON THE ROAD
ISBN 0-88129-025-3

A sequel to *The Wild Side.* Ride along with Datz in true-life adventures chasing stamp deals all over the map from the desolate hinterlands of Wyoming and Montana to the bright lights of Las Vegas and New York. An amazing odyssey: fast times and big-dollar deals, wild goose chases and third-rate motels, blizzards and tornadoes, eccentric millionaires and desert rats, even hippie hitchhikers. Action packed all the way. You'll be up all night finishing this one.

MORE GOOD READING
BY STEPHEN R. DATZ

THE BUYERS GUIDE
ISBN 0-88219-026-1

A **must** for every buyer of premium quality U.S. stamps. Covers every important U.S. stamp (more than 600) and includes: a stamp-by-stamp analysis of premium characteristics; gum and hinging; centering and margins; color and freshness; faults and imperfections; warnings about fakes and problem stamps; when to expertize; quantities NH vs. hinged; frequency at auction; completely illustrated. A powerhouse of knowledge—the kind professionals carry inside their heads—at your fingertips in a convenient, easy-to-use handbook.

STAMP INVESTING
ISBN 0-88219-029-6

The essential guide to profit in stamp investing. Includes: economics of the stamp market; basic strategies and tactics; speculative strategies; spotting profit opportunities; utilizing statistical tools; how and when to buy right—and sell right; stamp investment myths; Wall Street and stamps; scams and rip-offs to avoid; plus much more. If you enjoy stamps, there's no reason why you shouldn't profit from them, too.

Available wherever books are sold or visit
www.stephenrdatz.com

CPSIA information can be obtained at www.ICGtesting.com
Printed in the USA
LVOW05s2232191213

366155LV00012B/307/P